A Glimps

Imagining what Heaven is like

James Olah

OLAH Books

A Glimpse into Heaven

Imagining what Heaven is like

James Olah

©February 26, 2017
Revised 1-16-18; 7-24-18; 3-31-20; 12-20-21
All Rights Reserved

ISBN-13: 978-1544168074
ISBN-10: 1544168071

Imprint: Independently published

Website addresses recommended throughout this book offer resources for further study. Websites are not intended in any way to be or imply an endorsement, nor does the publisher vouch for their content.

The author has italicized Bible Verses to help them stand out. Bold is the author's emphasis on verses.

Scripture from the HOLY BIBLE, NEW INTERNATIONAL VERSION®, NIV®. Copyright © 1973, 1978, 1984, 2011, by Biblica, Inc. ™ Used by permission. All rights reserved worldwide.

Scripture quotes are taken from the World English Bible (WEB) and are in the Public Domain. It is part of the Online Bible, at http://www.onlinebible.net/ © 2008

Scripture from The Holy Bible, 21st Century King James Version (KJ21), Copyright 1994, Deuel Enterprises, Inc., Gary, SD 57237, and used by permission. 21st Century King James Version. It is part of the Online Bible and at http://www.onlinebible.net/

The Original Strong's Greek and Hebrew Lexicon is part of the Online Bible and at http://www.onlinebible.net/

OLAH Books

Dedication

To Nancy, my first wife,
who died of cancer after 43 years of marriage.
She was a wonderful wife, a good friend, a devoted
mother, and a faithful partner in ministry.

✽ ✽ ✽ ✽ ✽ ✽ ✽ ✽ ✽

"Since, then, you have been raised with Christ,
set your hearts on things above,
where Christ is, seated at the right hand of God.
Set your minds on things above, not on earthly things.
For you died, and your life
is now hidden with Christ in God.
When Christ, who is your life, appears,
then you also will appear with him in glory."
Colossians 3:1–4 (NIV)

Table of Contents

INTRODUCTION: Wondering about heaven

MY WIFE DIED after 43 years of marriage. I often contemplate what she is doing. Have you lost a loved one and experienced the same kind of thoughts? What are they doing in heaven? Do they miss us as much as we miss them? Are they content and enjoying life without us? What have you been wondering about heaven?

When people talk about heaven, they reference near-death experiences where someone meets Jesus, chats with family members, or speaks of the beauty, peace, or love they experience. These are claims people make about heaven. Are they real? It's possible. After all, the Apostle Paul had such an experience and saw heaven.[1] Once I hear these stories, my thoughts go to the following question: what happens after that? What will keep us occupied and keep life exciting 10,000 years from now? In his color trilogy (White, Black, Red), Ted Dekker presents God as an eternal babysitter entertaining his people with unique situations to which they continually look forward. Will our time be filled with productive times, or will we need to be entertained? This book explores possible ideas of what heaven may be like for the eons to come. What will make heaven an enjoyable existence? How will I be productive there? What will be the source of my worship and praise?

In writing this book, it is not my purpose to present wild ideas. I seek to use teachings and principles from Scripture as a basis for understanding the kinds of things that may happen as we settle in. I am proposing ideas that help us understand the daily activities we may enjoy in heaven. The purpose of this book is not to expound direct biblical teachings about heaven but to extract ideas about how God

---

[1] 2 Corinthians 12:1-5

5

made us that describe the kind of life we could live once we get there. We will not be idle but be active. Just as God told Adam in his innocence to work to develop the earth, so we too will work in heaven. My book has a different purpose. When we've been there 10,000 years, bright shining as the sun, what will we be doing to keep busy, learn about God, have fun, and keep our worship fresh and our relationship vibrant with God?

I want you to get excited about heaven by thinking about the possibilities of what it will be like when you get there. Paul challenged us to use our imagination, and scripture should continuously regulate those thoughts. *"However, as it is written: "No eye has seen, no ear has heard, **no mind has concei**ved what God has prepared for those who love him."*[2]

While writing this book, I spoke with friends about heaven. We shared our ideas, which caused us to get more excited about heaven. What is life like in heaven? Have you wondered about that at all? Anticipating heaven affects us now by giving hope and purpose in life, thus allowing this truth to motivate us in our current lives. *"Therefore, my dear brothers and sisters, stand firm. Let nothing move you. Always give yourselves fully to the work of the Lord because you know that your labor in the Lord is not in vain."*[3]

It makes sense that the more we know about our upcoming adventure, the more eager we will be to go home. Anticipating the good that God has prepared for us is the motivation to serve God. It seems like fewer Christians are talking about heaven. Where is their excitement? Are they afraid or embarrassed to identify with Jesus? Maybe some don't value their future hope. Such hope should motivate and encourage us in how we face life and share our faith with others.

Several years ago, a Christian song was popular on Christian and secular radio stations. It grabbed people's hearts because it seized their imaginations about this magnificent place. The song was "I Can Only

---

[2] 1 Corinthians 2:9 Emphasis added by author.
[3] 1 Corinthians 15:58

Imagine."[4] People liked it because the song encouraged them to envision heaven's existence by thinking of possibilities.

The material I present in this book comes from applying truths we don't usually associate with teaching about heaven. Also, I used my sanctified imagination as I contemplated and applied these Biblical teachings about how God designed us. The ideas I propose may help you think of our new homeland more realistically. No matter how splendid heaven is, it is still a foggy picture in our minds without ideas. Most of us have no idea of how to contemplate the glories of heaven. We anticipate it, yet we don't dig into God's word enough to form a legitimate picture of our future existence. Our desire for heaven should be a strong motivation in our life. This type of thinking is essential, for we won't talk about those things that we don't clearly understand. Even though we realize that Heaven is an excellent place, that does not convince all believers of how good it is. Having a more realistic picture of heaven in our mind allows us to talk to unbelievers with greater confidence and equips us to encourage believers and ourselves in times of loss.

Revelation 21-22 talks about the physical beauty of heaven. That's my future home, and hopefully yours. This scripture portion mentions facts about Heaven, such as who will or won't be there and a little of what we do, and there's an invitation to accept God's salvation so all can be there. However, when it comes to the specifics of what we will experience and do daily, the Bible says little.

In developing the teaching in my recent book on hell,[5] I took what the Bible said the believer has in salvation and counted it as a loss for those in hell. For example, the Christian has forgiveness of all sins; the non-reconciled person will experience the burning guilt of all their sins

---

[4] **I Can Only Imagine** was the first single recorded by Christian rock band MercyMe. Written and composed by Bart Millard. http://www.klove.com/music/artists/mercyme/songs/i-can-only-imagine-lyrics.aspx -This song was not the motivation for my book. I heard it and decided to include it while in the editing process.

5 "What in Hell is Happening" James Olah, Published in 2015 by OLAH Books. Distributors: Amazon Kindle, Create Space, iBook, Nook (Barns and Noble) Kobo, Oyster, Page Foundry, Scribd, Bibliotheca, and Tolino 24symbols.

for eternity. To get an idea of what kind of guilt they will experience, read about David and the guilt he felt after committing adultery with Bathsheba,[6] and the guilt Judas had after he betrayed Christ.[7] God will love the believer forever. When the non-reconciled person rejects God's salvation, they also reject His love. Therefore, they will not experience any aspect of God's love again. The children of God are full members of His family, but the non-reconciled will have no sense of belonging to anyone. These people will be alone with no one to care about them; and will not enjoy anyone's friendship for eternity. I used the 'learning by contrast" method to teach what the non-reconciled will experience in hell. This method is not apparent at first, but the more you think about it, the more sense such contrasts make.

The Bible does not say this is what the non-reconciled person will experience in hell, but we come to these conclusions by understanding what the Bible says about believers. Those in hell will enjoy none of the benefits that believers take for granted. When you recognize that, what the non-believer faces in hell becomes more apparent, even though the Bible does not directly address this reality.

To understand what the eternal state may be like, I describe heaven through stories. These stories will focus on the unique design of each human and those talents, abilities, and passions God gave us to bring Him glory. That which gives us the unique ability to honor God distinctively is our giftedness, passions, interests, creativity, and capabilities instilled in us at birth. It is logical to imagine being completely free to employ these qualities after He removes all the effects of sin. We are then free to become the person God intended and enjoy intimate fellowship with God as we get to know and serve Him.

---

[6] "Wash away all my iniquity and cleanse me from my sin. For I know my transgressions, **and my sin is always before me**." Psalm 51:2-3 (Emphasis mine.)

[7] "When Judas, who had betrayed him, saw that Jesus was condemned, **he was seized with remorse** and returned the thirty pieces of silver to the chief priests and the elders. 4 "I have sinned," he said, "for I have betrayed innocent blood." Matthew 27:3-4. David and Judas' statements describe the way guilt will grab each person who must bear their own guilt. "*My sin is always before me.*" That means he couldn't get it out of his mind. -- "*He was seized with remorse*" Judas realized what a terrible thing he did. Will not all in hell recognize what a terrible thing they did in offending God and rejecting salvation?

Every year millions of people wait for their families to gather for Christmas. They celebrate, give gifts, feast, have fun, and reminisce. If our earthly celebrations are grand, then heaven will be superior. If you have a hard time imagining what life may be like in heaven, then I think you will enjoy this book. The more we think about the possibilities of Heaven, the more we will eagerly anticipate our eternal home.

My friend Tracy helps with some of my editing. When she finished editing this book, she wrote me a comment that expresses a response that I hope you will discover as well.

"I am excited about heaven in a whole new way. You have opened my mind to the possibilities because you have a fresh approach to heaven. I like your use of Scripture throughout the book to back up your teachings. I've never read anything quite like this. I was already okay with dying. I mean, I know life in heaven is greater than anything we have experienced here, but the idea that God would continue to use our gifts in heaven is exciting. I love to sing, but anymore I sing like a frog. I'm looking forward to singing with the choirs of angels with a perfect voice. My Grief-Share[8] group just finished the section on heaven. I told them how your book changed my outlook on the possibilities of heaven. They all want to read it."

It is my prayer that this book will so inspire you about heaven.

Are you ready to get started? Follow me as I tag along with one of the main characters in the book. It is my first wife, Nancy. I present her life and death to give an example of the kind of things that may characterize life in heaven. The next chapter will provide some details about her. I pop in and out of the story to give you a first-person perspective. You will also meet my angel friend, Asriel. I think you will like how the story comes together from an angel's perspective.

---

8 Leading GriefShare seminars and support groups are people who understand what you are going through and want to help. You'll gain access to valuable GriefShare resources to help you recover from your loss and look forward to rebuilding your life. If you or a loved one is facing grief, this is an excellent program. Check it out at https://www.griefshare.org/about

After publishing this book, some have asked me if the content came about due to personal dreams or visions. No, I find it easier to incorporate stories, using people I know, into the book's teaching. Placing myself in the story is a convenient way to develop the instructional portion of the book, as in chapter two. I think stories are easy to follow and make the teaching of truth more interesting.

Paul directs us to think about heavenly things and what is waiting for us. Let me also challenge you to contemplate what heaven is like for at least a week. What implications can you draw from these verses for your life?

"Set your minds on things above, not on earthly things.
For you died, and your life is now hidden with Christ in God."[9]
"But our citizenship is in heaven. And we eagerly await
a Savior from there, the Lord Jesus Christ."[10]

I pray, along with Paul, that the eyes of your heart may be enlightened so that you may know the hope to which he has called *you, the riches of his glorious inheritance in his holy people.*[11]

* * * * * * * * * * * *

"I have come home at last! This is my real country! I belong here. This is the land I have been looking for all my life, though I never knew it till now... Come further up, come further in!"
— **C.S. Lewis, The Last Battle**
* * * * * * * * * * * *

*But our citizenship is in heaven, and from it, we await a Savior, the Lord Jesus Christ -- **Philippians 3:20***
* * * * * * * * * * * *

For the Christian, heaven is where Jesus is. We do not need to speculate on what heaven will be like. It is enough to know that we will be forever with Him.
William Barclay

---

9 Colossians 3:2
10 Philippians 3:20
11 Ephesians 1:18

Chapter One -- Nancy Goes Home

I speak about the death of my wife, Nancy, effortlessly. However, facing her death was not easy. Thinking about life without Nancy and the loss of her companionship was beyond my comprehension. We take that familiarity of our partners for granted until they are gone. The pain of their absence takes you to your limits at times. Loneliness and lack of companionship are like suddenly missing a part of your body. You no longer feel whole without them.

I want to share with you my account of the days leading up to the home-going of Nancy. This account will set the stage for developing the rest of this book.

I WAS MARRIED TO NANCY for more than 43 years. It was December when we met in the girl's dorm at college. We hit it off well and married a year and a half later. It was the month after I graduated. Over the years, we served the Lord together in two youth pastorates.

Following my service as a youth pastor, I accepted a call to Port Huron, Michigan, to be the senior pastor of a church where we served for 16 years. We then received an invitation to pastor a church in Davison, Michigan. I was a pastor there for 18 years. Nancy was by my side all those years, serving as we celebrated, served, and helped deal with people's difficulties and life struggles. We taught, prayed with, comforted many of our people, and had great fellowship with them over those years. Entertaining people and missionaries in our home were our delights. Nancy was an organizer in the children's ministries. Being a teacher, she trained many who worked with her. She loved teaching women's Bible studies because this allowed her to dig deeper into God's word. She was a shy woman until you came to know her, and then she could hold her own in any conversation. She had a keen wit and was an intelligent woman. One of her favorite sayings was, "This too shall pass," and sure enough, most problems did. We had two wonderful daughters, and we enjoyed taking yearly vacations with our family. Camping provided many great memories especially sitting around the campfire many evenings, making toaster pies and smores. My parents lived in Florida, so we also took many trips to visit. Nancy made our house a home and was the motivation behind our fun-filled celebrations. It was her inspiration that pulled the family together. We enjoyed many good friendships with our people through the years that will be precious to us throughout eternity.

I retired at the end of October 2011. In mid-December of that year, she went in for an ultrasound, and the doctor discovered that Nancy had cancer. Because she had health issues over the last year, it was almost a relief to learn the nature of her problem. Even though cancer is a terrible disease, we knew that we could deal with it with the Lord's help. We experienced something we didn't expect. It was the overwhelming presence of God's peace in our lives. I'll tell you more about that at the end of the chapter. The Christmas holiday prevented her from getting the next cancer test. They scheduled her PET scan by mid-January. This test detects cancer and helps understand the stage of one's disease.

We learned that Nancy's cancer was stage four a few days later. It started in her kidney and metastasized to her bones, lungs, and brain. In mid-December, we learned that Nancy had cancer. A month later, we learned that it was terminal. The doctor gave her 12-14 months to live at that time and maybe a couple of months longer with Chemo. By the end of the month, they started her course of treatment. We anticipated having at least a year together.

Our oldest daughter became engaged in January. They were planning to be married the following October. She wanted to make sure her mom would be strong enough to be at the wedding, so she moved it to April. Nancy met Heather's fiancée, Grahame, and she liked him. She anticipated the wedding, which gave us great joy amid this most difficult trial.

When people talk about how they go through that time when one has a terminal disease, the responses vary greatly. Some won't talk about it because that makes it more real. It was one of the most precious times of our life for Nancy and me. It was not because she had cancer, but because of the closeness and love we experienced with one another during that time. We talked about everything. We talked about our lives together and our ministry experiences. We talked about how God richly blessed us with wonderful daughters and grandchildren who stole our hearts. We talked about what it would be like to die and then what it would be like to walk into the presence of Jesus for the first time. We talked about our children and grandchildren. They meant so much to us. We communicated what we wanted to say to them. We also spoke about my future without her and her desire for me. We anticipated the people she would meet in heaven who were already there. My dad and her mom went to heaven years before. There were many dear friends and relatives that died over the years who would welcome her.

I recently talked to a person about the times I moved from one church to another. Each time I resigned from a church, I noticed a difference in our communication. When talking with church members, I discovered we only talked about the past and present, but little of our conversation was about the future. However, when I resigned from each church, I noticed during that month before I left, I had less to talk about with the people. That's because we were no longer talking future. Even though we talked about getting together after Nancy and I left, few followed through. Therefore, after my resignation, the dynamics of our communication changed. There is something about having a future to talk about that gives a vibrance to conversations.

When we learned that Nancy would die shortly, our conversation did not go flat but was even more alive. We both realized that there would only be an interruption in our relationship. We would see each other once again. Anticipating our future reunion, not as husband and wife,[12] but as two people with a special bond, gave our conversation depth and kept it alive.

---

12 "At the resurrection, people will neither marry nor be given in marriage; they will be like the angels in heaven." Matthew 22:30

13

About five weeks after we learned Nancy had terminal cancer, we had to take her to the hospital. Her strength had so drained that day she could not get out of her chair. We thought it might have been the effects of the chemo. We thought she might need adjustments to her medication, or perhaps it was dehydration. Little did we know that on that Saturday evening, when the ambulance took her to Genesys Hospital in Grand Blanc, Michigan, that this would become her departure point for heaven. Nancy was feeling a little better on Sunday. I would say that Monday was a noticeable improvement from my perspective. However, on Monday evening, she got exhausted during visitation. We all decided to leave so she could get a good night's rest.

The next day when I returned, I expected improvement from the night before. I thought she would be more alert and ready to talk. To my dismay, she was not responding or talking. From that day on, she continued to decline.

We always appreciated our good friends and family relationships. It was encouraging to have them be with us in the hospital room. There was a time of talking, laughing, reminiscing, and praying. Having people stand with us in these challenging times was invaluable. I knew each of them loved Nancy and me. They wanted us to know how much they cared.

Nancy declined over the week. On Thursday evening, the nurses moved her from a regular room to the hospice wing. The days dragged on, and there was no improvement, no response. We came to grips with the certainty of her imminent death during that time. In dealing with the reality of death, there comes a time when we are ready to say to God, "Lord, I release her to you. Your will be done."

Saturday vigil was ending as friends went home, followed by my daughters leaving together. At around 10:30 PM, they returned to our home in Davison. Since Tuesday, I have slept in the room with Nancy. After everything quieted down, I would email people about updates, and before bed, I would talk and pray with Nancy. Communication was so important to us through the years, and I didn't want it to end.

14

I think it was around 11:15 that Nancy's breathing started to change. I talked with the nurses, and as a result, I called my daughters to return. I wanted them there when Nancy left on her journey to heaven. They weren't home very long when I called. They hurried back. It was about a half-hour return trip. By the time they arrived, Nancy's breathing had become shallower and less frequent. Our daughters were there less than half an hour when Nancy took her last breath that allowed her to start on the next leg of her journey into a new life.

We cried together and then prayed. I thanked God for loaning her to me, and for the good times we had, and for the great hope that we have because of Jesus Christ. It was a celebration. Our cries were not of desperation but the departure of a friend who would no longer walk this life's journey with us. We didn't know the next time we would see her. Our life now goes on without her love and support. We experienced a hope-filled sadness and loss.

We called people. I emailed the family about Nancy's departure. We notified the nurse and let them know that Allen Funeral Home would take Nancy's body. Despite the confusion that comes at such a time, we had God's hope and confidence about where she was as we walked out of the hospital together, our family minus one.

Heidi's story about Nancy

My daughter Heidi wrote her thoughts about that event. She read this at Nancy's funeral. I want to share it with you because even though we have confidence that our saved loved ones go to heaven, there is still grief and struggles at their death. Perhaps her description of the event will encourage you as well.

February 26, 2012 - 12:25 AM -- Sunday morning

Mama is safely in the arms of Jesus.

We prayed for healing, and God has given her the ultimate healing ~ a brand new body!

No more pain! A first for her.

I never experienced watching someone die. In the last few days, my stomach was in knots for fear of seeing mom take her last breath. I kept telling God that I couldn't watch my mother die. However, being the ever-gentle God, He is, I knew He would wrap his arms around me and whisper, "I am here."

Heather and I returned home for the night. We weren't home long when dad called us and said we should come back because Mama's breathing changed. While driving back to the hospital, I felt completely calm. I said everything to Mama that I could before we left. I expressed my love, gave her my permission, and encouraged her to let us go.

As Heather and I walked into the hospital, I started praying for a miracle. I needed to see Jesus in her Home-going. I wanted to find peace and God with her final breath.

We reached her room, room 2161. Dad was right; her breathing had changed. Heather and I positioned ourselves by mom. All I could do was speechlessly take in the scene. Dad was caressing mom's forehead, and Mom looked so peaceful. Dad was quietly expressing his love repeatedly to her. I held her hand as I did for the past three days and watched. God's holy presence was in the room. It was overwhelmingly peaceful. I stood in awe and was taken aback by the

16

beauty of what was happening. My mama was meeting Jesus! She and I talked many times about that moment and what it would be like to stand in His presence. Because of the unknown, it was a bit scary.

However, I saw no fear, no anxiety on my Mama's face before me. Just peace.

We recognized when her spirit left her. My dad immediately started praying, committing her to God the Father, and praising Him for who He is.

We were standing on Holy Ground.

I just saw God do an incredible miracle!

I didn't cry. I couldn't. I just saw Jesus, and I was in awe! Incredible Peace filled that room. Dad cried for a bit. I couldn't take my eyes off what I had just beheld. A Beautiful Home-Going!

I'm the one who went out to inform the nurse. I was calm as ever. I found a nurse and quietly told her my mom had passed. She came into the room to verify it and said she had gone peacefully. After she left, we made some calls. I didn't have too many to make, so I was able to stand by my mom and stare into the most beautiful face I had ever seen. She was with God! I kissed her forehead for a long moment. Then I told her to drink long at the Living Water!

My dad started contacting his family. He was incredible to watch, so strong yet weak and vulnerable. God was carrying him, just as He was carrying Heather and me.

My final moments with mom were sitting and holding her hand. God gently reminded me: "To be absent from the body is to be present with the Lord." This verse kept running through my mind as I soaked in the beauty of my mom and the reality of that truth.

My Mama was finally Home!

As we left her room, I didn't feel the dread that I thought I would. We said goodbye to our nurse. She commented that she had never seen a family so at peace before. We told her that Mama was with her Savior, and she is now divinely healed!

As we walked out to the car, a few tears fell down my cheeks as I had to walk away from my Mama, my best friend, forever here on earth. However, God is faithful and kind. I will see her again someday. THAT is what ultimate Home feels like, looks like, and IS like.

Heidi Jones

God's Peace

Nancy and I experienced God's peace immediately after learning she had cancer. Neither of us understood how or why we experienced such overwhelming peace. I did not know how to explain it to people. God's peace captivated our being dramatically during the next nine weeks. I spoke of that peace often as I talked with friends about our experience, but it was not until recently, as I was reading a book, that I finally understood why we had this peace. This peace sustained us and allowed us to focus our trust on God rather than on fear as we walked through our troubled waters of the unknown.

This peace sustained us and allowed us to focus our complete trust on God rather than on fear as we walked into our unknown, troubled waters.

Peace does not remove the hurt of loss. Those who lose a loved one know the emptiness in their hearts and souls that engulf them in grief. I have a saying that I use to describe loneliness. "Loneliness is everything it's cracked up to be." Peace does not exempt you from an emotional response, but it does stabilize your inner being during this time.

Why did we have this peace? It was not a fluke but based on a legitimate premise. Even though more aspects of our relationship brought about this peace, three truths stand out. I attribute our peace to three vital elements that God used to sustain both of us. Concrete provides a stable foundation for a building. The three components in concrete are gravel, water, and cement. The peace that gave us a firm foundation has three elements as well. These elements established the grounds upon which we lived before this happened and then had a profound effect, unexpectedly, as we went through this life-shaking event.

Bible

The first element is that Nancy and I knew the Word of God. Over the years, we read the Bible, studied the Bible, memorized Bible verses, and sat under the teaching of good Bible teachers. I taught and preached every week; at my first church four times a week and at the next church three times a week. We took the Bible seriously and sought to live by its truths, and encouraged others by it. The Bible is not just a book to be taught but lived. I'm not saying you have to be in God's word as much as I was, but it is essential to regularly be in God's word and seek to understand it. We didn't read the Bible as a good luck charm. In other words, we didn't believe that reading the Bible prevented terrible things from happening or gave us a good day if we did read it. Reading the Bible was not automatic protection from the problems of life. That is superstition, not faith in God, nor is that an expression of a relationship with God. The Bible teaches us how to live. We chose to live that way. Scripture teaches us about God and what He's like, which opens the door to establish a relationship with Him and trust Him. That was a regular part of our life over the years. It was not enough to read the Bible, but we sought to know it in a way that would affect how we view life and develop our relationship with God. The Bible was the basis of our life.

Heaven

Secondly, we recognized heaven as a real place to desire. Our final destination is heaven. God sets the time for our arrival. Yes, leaving for heaven was difficult for Nancy and me, as well as for those who love us. We had absolute confidence that heaven was our final destination when we died. Heaven was a reality we both anticipated. Jesus is there. We know He will be with us and take care of us. I was sending Nancy to a much better place and entrusting her to someone who explicitly loves her. I knew my time was coming that I would join her in heaven, not as her husband but as a good friend. The reality of heaven and being with God gave us the hope we needed to face the end of Nancy's life. It did not stop at Nancy's death. The reality of heaven helped me deal with my grief. I especially enjoyed the Gaither Home Coming Singers and the wonderful thoughts of heaven they present through their songs. In my heartache, I sang along with them and cried as I thought about Nancy and God's faithfulness.

Relationship with God

The third ingredient in our foundation was that we both developed a genuine relationship with God. We knew Him, trusted our Friend, and loved Him. He never promised us that we would always understand why things happen, but He gave us peace when we didn't understand why. This peace passes all understanding. Jesus was our friend. When I visit a friend, it is to enjoy each other. We had joy in our relationship with Jesus. We served Jesus, loved Him, and He revealed Himself to us in life. He was no stranger but a trusted friend. Therefore, when we heard the news of cancer, we knew Jesus would walk with us through this. When Jesus took her home, we had absolute confidence in her well-being with Him.

Peace

Nancy and I had the freedom to enjoy our time together, talk freely, and have confidence about the future because of God's peace. Such peace doesn't come easily or without a cost. It took time, patience, and energy to get to know God and that He is faithful to His word. Over time, we built our relationship with this One, who proved He is a trusted friend. As we faced life's trials and looked back, we noticed how He helped us. This history with Him gave us confidence in His faithfulness, strengthening our relationship with Him. Our hope of heaven and its grandeur, along with our assurance[13] of going there, were foundational elements that made our lives secure and resilient. These truths became second nature to us, gave us peace during our trials, and allowed us to continue to walk in a relationship with God. That allowed us to trust Him in the unknown, as well as have an understanding of His ways. Through the experiences of our life, our

---

[13] "And this is the testimony: God has given us eternal life, and this life is in his Son. Whoever has the Son has life; whoever does not have the Son of God does not have life. I write these things to you who believe in the name of the Son of God so that you may know that you have eternal life." 1 John 5:11-13

Lord proved Himself reliable. These are the reasons that God's peace surrounded both of us during Nancy's dying process. Peace of heart does not come from a formula but from a relationship built over time. I'm merely offering you tools to help you develop your relationship with God.

The Bible describes the peace we experience as the *"Peace that passes all understanding."*[14] People agonize over why certain things happen or why God allows a tragedy to occur. Why did God permit my loved one to die? When calamity comes to some, it paralyzes the progress in their faith or prevents them from serving the Lord or drawing closer to Him. Even when we don't understand why things happen, we can still have God's peace. It goes beyond reason; it transcends our understanding and thus allows us to trust God and know there is a purpose beyond our consideration.

I don't know why God took my wife when He did. I didn't know how her death would affect my life. Did I grieve, and was I hurting? Absolutely! However, I also had peace amid my sorrow. During that time, I continued to grow in my faith and relationship with God. God's peace; how wonderful it is.

* * * * * * * * *

"Since, then, you have been raised with Christ,
set your hearts on things above,
where Christ is, seated at the right hand of God.
Set your minds on things above, not on earthly things.
For you died, and your life
is now hidden with Christ in God.
When Christ, who is your life, appears,
then you also will appear with him in glory."
Colossians 3:1–4 (NIV)

---

[14] Philippians 4:7

Chapter Two -- An Image that Endures

SINCE NANCY DIED, THE YEARS caused me to think more about heaven. My strong desire was to understand eternity more fully. We know heaven will express God's glory, but what will make it great, and how will we relate to Him? That naturally led me to consider what life will be like in heaven in the eons to come. I don't understand vague concepts. I need something that gives me the kind of details my mind can start to grasp. Indeed, God wants us to think correctly about heaven. Specifics help us visualize the reality of what we have not yet seen. My thoughts could scarcely go beyond the first few days of eternity. What would make the rest of eternity so exciting? I wanted to know what kind of activities would occupy us in heaven that will continue to be satisfying, energizing, and inspiring. Since God is in charge, what kind of innovative ideas and activities does He have in mind to help us have a continual growing experience that could last for an eternity?

Writing about the afterlife is not new to me. A couple of years earlier, I wrote a book on hell. However, because of changes in my life, I was not yet ready to write a book on heaven. That is until last year when God laid it on my heart to start my next writing project. It was the right time in my life to deal with this subject of heaven in more depth. When I began focusing my heart and mind on eternity, ideas about the specific nature of heaven started to flood my thoughts. Before Christmas of 2016, I started putting my ideas into writing, and the topics of this book seemed to come into focus. That is when this book began taking shape.

I preached on heaven many times over the years. I often shared a few thoughts about Heaven in the funeral services of believers but didn't have a lot of time to go in-depth. I wanted something with more substance. I wondered what my focus should be in writing this book.

Most books take the specific teachings of Scripture to describe heaven. Others share their near-death experiences. In the process of developing this book, I wondered what we were missing biblically in our thinking about eternity. While considering heaven, I returned to one recurring theme that made a lot of sense. Allow me to tell you what that theme is through the following story.[15]

My Opportunity

HIS NAME WAS ASRIEL. God sent this angel with a message for me. I could hardly believe my eyes when he appeared. Why did God send me an angel? I stood stunned for a moment before Asriel said anything. All the while, he was smiling at my bewilderment in anticipation of delivering his message. I think he took pleasure in my confusion. I wondered if all angels were like him in having a sense of humor during times like this. When I calmed down, he began to speak.

With excitement in his voice, he proceeded to inform me that God was offering me the opportunity of a lifetime. I was offered an audience with Jesus if I accepted. He said He would discuss one topic with me. I can ask as many questions relating to that topic as I want during our one-hour meeting. He does not do this often, so I should feel honored that He selected me. He knows how eager I am to learn about heaven and my desire to have people better informed about the positive aspects of heaven. He wants me to feel confident about the direction of my book.

"Pardon me. I haven't properly introduced myself. My name is Asriel. I know about you because your wife Nancy spoke of you when I escorted her to heaven."

"You did? Will you tell me how she's doing?"

---

[15] Some people asked if this was an actual event I experienced. I composed this story for the sake of making the book more personal. Besides, I thought it would be fun to think about what it would be like to speak with Jesus face to face.

"I can't do that now, Jim, because I have another mission. Do you want to discuss a topic with Jesus or not?"

"I sure do. I'll have eternity to catch up with what's been happening with Nancy. I'll have to wait like everyone else."

"You know God is taking care of her, so that should set your mind at ease. Let's focus on the reason I'm here. You will meet Jesus in a dream. Limit your discussion to one topic, so formulate your best questions that define your subject. You have three days to prepare for your interview.

As soon as he finished his final statement, Asriel was gone. "I wondered *how he did that. Those angels are really something!*" I then sat down to think about my topic and the questions I would focus on in my discussion with Jesus. During the rest of the evening, I thought, prayed, and wrote out topic ideas to use in my interview. After all, I wanted a good conversation. I contemplated my choices carefully over the next few days, and by the time I was ready to go to bed the third night, I had my questions fixed firmly in my mind about heaven. As I waited to fall asleep, I eagerly anticipated my dream in which I would meet Jesus. Excitement gripped my heart as I awaited my meeting. I also noticed that I wasn't afraid. The fact of the matter is that we had become such good friends over the years; I could not think of any reason to fear Him or be nervous.

As I was lying in bed, my mind was going a mile a minute. I thought, *"I will never get to sleep."* I rehearsed my questions several times in my mind to make sure I formulated them well. I could not turn off my thinking. Then before I knew it, I seamlessly entered a deep sleep.

I awoke with a start, finding myself standing before Jesus. He had a big warm grin when He greeted me.

"I'm delighted to have you here. I just wanted to encourage you in your heaven project and help you explore some important aspects. I knew that if you depended on the Holy Spirit, you would determine relevant questions. We have little time, so let's get started with the questions you have for me."

I stood there for a moment drinking in His beauty. He was awesome! My heart filled with awe in his presence. I blinked a couple of times and stammered as I normally do when I don't know exactly how to start. Then without further hesitation, the question just popped out of my mouth.

Why are humans special?

"Jesus, why is humanity so special to you? You set your love on us, redeemed us, brought believers into your family, and even provided us a home in heaven so that we could be with you. What makes us so important that you choose to honor us so richly?[16]"

"Jim, your question is very perceptive; when humanity understands how we made them in creation, as well as what we provided for them in redemption, then they will realize an essential part of their purpose on earth that will continue to play out in eternity.

"That which makes humans special and valuable is that we created humanity in our image. Even though birds, fish, and animals have life, along with different abilities, man is far superior because we made them in our image."[17]

"I know that is why we are important, but I'm asking you to explain your image in a way I can better understand its implications in eternity. My thought is that the more we understand how you created us, the better equipped we are to face life. Also, if

---

[16] "*I pray that the eyes of your heart may be enlightened in order that you may know the hope to which he has called you, the riches of his glorious inheritance in his holy people.*" Ephesians 1:18

[17] Then God said, "Let us make mankind in our image, in our likeness, so that they may rule over the fish in the sea and the birds in the sky, over the livestock and all the wild animals, and over all the creatures that move along the ground." So God created mankind in his own image, in the image of God he created them; male and female he created them. Genesis 1:26-27 See also: Romans 8:29; Colossians 3:10; James 3:9.

I'm not mistaken, that helps us to understand what life will be like in heaven with you."

"You've been doing some critical thinking Jim. I am delighted to share the implications of what it means that we created humanity in our image."

"Jesus, you know I'm a little slow on the uptake sometimes, so make it simple and don't go too fast."

"I know just what you need, Jim, for I understand your communication method and learning style. Remember, I designed you. You will be able to follow me and completely remember what I said. I'm also eager for this conversation with you."

I was feeling comfortable with Jesus. It meant a lot to me to know that He understood everything about me and related to me on a level where I didn't feel threatened. What a joy it was to be in this exchange with my Maker.

The image of God

"There are many qualities humanity has because of being created in my image. Most have no idea how they are experiencing actual God-qualities in their life.

"Humanity's fall and resulting sinfulness have corrupted their ability to express the divine nature fully, even though our image is still in them. That is why even bad people do good things and can benefit humanity. As a result, you can find good even in the worst of people. In redemption, I restore the believer with the ability to express our nature more fully.[18] Those who reject my salvation will never experience the joy of expressing our image that resides in them. They will only have a burning desire to express that part

---

[18] 2 Peter 1:4 "Through these he has given us his very great and precious promises, so that through them you may participate in the divine nature, having escaped the corruption in the world caused by evil desires."

of our image. I'm glad you mentioned that in your book on hell, Jim."

He continued. "The foundational truth about our image in humanity is that we placed in them intellect, emotions, and free will as well as the ability to enter an ever-growing relationship with us. These qualities are superior to that which we implanted in animals. Even though animals have some of these characteristics, they cannot progress to higher levels of those qualities given to humanity. You don't find animals increasing in their intellect, emotions, or will. Birds of a feather still sing the same song, build the same kind of nests, mate in the same way, and scavenge for food as they always have. There has been little or no change since I created them.

Intellect

"Humans, on the other hand, can grow and increase in these abilities and use them in thousands of diverse ways. Their intellect allows them to learn the hidden treasures we put in creation, life, and developing relationships. Whereas humans only use a small percentage of their brainpower now, they will continue to grow in their mental capacity in the eons to come. Their new capability allows them to delve into greater depths of understanding the mind of God and the details of His creation. Intelligence is just one element that enables humans to develop meaningful relationships and communicate complex ideas. Those who don't have high mental capacity are also very limited in communicating complex ideas and having meaningful conversations. To compensate for this, we gave many of them a big heart of love to make up for their lack of intellectual ability. Intelligence allows humans to converse, sing, write, build, be creative and artistic, and express complex ideas. Jim, this book you are writing is such an expression of our creativity in you.

"Intellect allows humans to make rational decisions. Sometimes people think that we should make all their decisions for them. As they come to know us and understand our hearts, we like to have them venture out on their own and use their reason to make wise decisions. They have the Word of God[19] to guide them and their experience of walking with us. Hence, we sometimes stand back and let them apply our word and make their own decisions. We love to watch them work through their reasoning process, even though they wonder why it seems we have gone silent on them. As they do this, they take ownership of our values, which helps them mature in their thinking process, which causes them to grow in their faith. The result is that they enter into a better understanding of our thinking process.

Emotions

"Our image includes a wide variety of emotions. They include the ability to experience joy[20], happiness, laughter, and excitement. Certain aspects of love allow you to feel a diversity of emotions. Think about the experience of loving your wife and the delight she brought you. You had fun with her, and you enjoyed happiness together. You were encouraged and challenged through your friendship. As you observed your children and grandchildren, you delighted in their antics and the growing process as they developed. These kinds of emotions are all part of our image in you. We understand such feelings and want you to experience that aspect of love. I know it is evident that the quality of love comprises various elements of our image in you. Both emotions and intellect are imperative in getting to know a person. Your feelings help draw you close to give relationships a certain excitement, and your will is the part that commits to the other.

We look forward to the emotional aspect of you getting to know us and experiencing the opening of your mind and abilities. We will laugh together and take joy in one another."

---

[19] 2 Timothy 3:16-17 (NIV) "All Scripture is God-breathed and is useful for teaching, rebuking, correcting and training in righteousness, so that the servant of God may be thoroughly equipped for every good work."

[20] John 15:11 "I have spoken these things to you, that my joy may remain in you, and that your joy may be made full."

"Jim, on another note, I know you enjoy a good humorous story?"

"I always enjoy entertaining stories, especially when there are unexpected twists. It sure adds a fun dimension to life. So, will there be humor in heaven too?"

"Your emotions allow you to enjoy humor and heart-stirring stories. I think you will enjoy the Humorous Story Night we have every week at Smile Stadium. We have experienced those humorous and touching incidents in people's lives as they took place. The Father and I smile with delight and laugh many times as we see the plot of our story unfold for them and the thrill that comes to their heart.

"Humans love discovering something new. Such discovery gets many excited, making them giddy as they jump around. That's a fun emotion we placed in them. Singing is an expression of one's heart, and songs come to life with feelings. The same is true of storytelling. We placed feelings in you to color how you look at life and interpret situations. In heaven, you will enjoy the perfect expression of your emotions. Think about telling a story without feelings. It is like the lines in a coloring book, drab and just waiting for color. Telling that same story with passion brings the picture to life, full of color that grabs your attention and makes it pleasurable. We gave you emotions to color your life. Eternity will have its share of pleasurable emotions.

Free Will

"We gave humanity a will which provides them with the power to initiate, to create, and to decide the direction of their life. Free will allows them to choose what they do, even if they want a relationship with us. Not only can they select heaven, but also hell. It is amid life's difficulties and struggles that they experience pain, death, disaster, disease, sickness, losses, unfair treatment, abandonment, and a myriad of other harmful or good things in which people have the option of seeing us or closing their minds to us. They can choose to live by faith and believe in my goodness, or they can close their eyes to us and believe in themselves and their inability and decide to walk away from us.

One's free will continues to be a vital driving force in heaven. Humanity will continue to use free will to make decisions, and by it, choose the way they want to honor me or glorify my Father. They will select the activities or direction of studies about us they wish to engage. Their constant motivation will always be the desire to honor and glorify us in all they learn and discover. We want them to discover everything they can about us, as they are involved in activities through eternity. That significant aspect of heaven will be a constant source of pleasure and purpose.

Eternal

"There is another quality that separates humans from animals. It is the fact that the human soul is eternal because of our image. Human life continues forever. That is good for the believer because that enables them to spend eternity in heaven with us in a dynamic, fulfilling relationship. However, the person who rejects reconciliation will experience the consequences to their soul for eternity.[21] Everyone exists for all eternity. It will not be pleasant for some, for they will exist with no hope of ever having any relationship with us. Never will they experience our favor because their rejection places them under eternal condemnation.[22] Being an immortal soul makes every single person essential and valuable. Every human has infinite worth, yet many view this precious quality with contempt in how they treat each other and dispose of those they deem 'unfit or unwanted' souls. The world has suffered from slavery, senseless wars, abortions, and the expression of hatred.

[21] Matthew 25:46 In speaking about the non-reconciled He says: *"These will go away into eternal punishment, but the righteous into eternal life."* Jesus uses the same Greek word when speaking about both punishment as well as life.

[22] John 3:18 (NIV) *"Whoever believes in him is not condemned, but whoever does not believe stands condemned already because they have not believed in the name of God's one and only Son."*

"Jim, are you following me so far? I don't want to go too fast and leave you in the dust. Man's intellect gives him the ability to discover and get to know us. His emotions give him delight and passion in his pursuits and relationships. His free will allows him to choose to have or reject a relationship with us for eternity, determine how they will treat others and how they seek to honor us."

"Yes, I'm following your train of thought very well. It makes good sense. By the way, I noticed your emotion. The excitement in your voice says this is important to you. I also am fascinated that you are enthusiastic when you talk about humanity. I seldom think about you getting excited about us and how you desire such good things for us."

"Jim, I am passionate about this because I gave my life for humanity to restore them to a full relationship with me and my Father. Our desire is for humankind to enjoy fellowship with us on the deepest level. In my love for humanity, I chose to suffer the worst possible expression of wrath from man, as well as by my Father. As you know, I willingly suffered because of their sin. I love all humanity, and I want them to choose to follow me so they can experience our life and be in an intimate relationship with us rather than be slaves to their flawed understanding of life. Even though we know what is best for them, we respect their free will and allow them the freedom to either reject or accept reconciliation with us. Since we are talking about emotions, I trust you recall Hebrews 12:2 that declare my motivation for dying on the cross. It was *"for the joy set before me that I endured the cross, disregarding its shame."* We are committed to welcoming people into a relationship with us.

Creative

"Let's get back on track, Jim. We made humanity in our image. We gave them a great variety of avenues to express our image. One that tops the list is our creative ability. Creativity allows them to develop ideas and implement them. Jim, I remember when you went to the Henry Ford Museum. You noticed the many ideas people had for building cars, sewing machines, vacuum cleaners, and the many inventions. People's creative ideas continued the improvement of each device. Our creativity in them captured their desire and ability to make changes and develop ideas.

"Creativity is also expressed through people's problem-solving skills as they build massive structures, as doctors practice medicine, as counselors help people and as pastors preach the Word. We implanted our image in all humanity. It saddens us to see man's creativity squelched by overly critical people who suppress creativity through their crushing control or malevolence. Then some rulers subjugate their people or refuse education to specific groups within their society to subdue their creativity. Sometimes, friends or family are overly critical or belittled through name-calling or demeaning comments.

"What good is creativity without talents and abilities to develop these ideas? Some people are visionaries. They see innovative possibilities but cannot always carry out their dreams. They need people gifted in other ways to surround them with the required skills, talents, and abilities to carry out their projects. That same kind of gifting will continue in heaven. We have gifted humanity to express their talents in a million different ways to help them use their inspiration for beneficial purposes. These talents and abilities flourish where there is the freedom to exercise them. Even suppressed people use their innate creativity. Creatively using abilities and skills allows them to improve in remarkable ways. You have no idea how the expertise of people thrived before the flood when humans lived 600-900 years. The sad thing is that those who pursue evil pervert good and became more creative in expressing evil.

"Many fail to transfer the idea of this teaching from their lifestyle on earth to the way they think about how they will live in heaven. When people get to heaven, they will continue to develop their creativity, talents, and abilities while increasing their skills all through eternity. Think about this, Jim. We equipped humanity

with these expressions of us. Why would we have humanity lay aside those wonderful qualities when they get to heaven? That expression of our image is going to add untold excitement and anticipation for them through their eternal existence."

"However, sad to say, while on earth, some don't value their talents or abilities. They squander them on petty things rather than wise investments. Some bury their gifts because they are afraid to put them into a useful expression. Others use them only to make a living and don't appreciate how we endowed them to know and serve us and humanity. It saddened us to see people making career decisions solely on how much money they could make rather than how they could develop the abilities we bestowed on them. Their self-centeredness causes them to focus on themselves rather than thinking of how much joy they could have in developing the talents and abilities we implanted in them. Many believers fail to see how they can use their talents and abilities to honor us."

Morality

"I am holy and cannot tolerate sin, so when Adam transgressed my command, that broke man's relationship with us. Sin has expressed itself in every kind of untold evil. I cannot and will not allow evil into my heaven.[23] Each person must receive forgiveness and cleansing from me to gain my acceptance and become my children."

"You cannot understand the image of God if you don't recognize the moral image we placed in you. Every person is a moral being. When a person is born from above, they can become righteous and just on earth. I will write my morality in their hearts, and it will be their constant code of conduct.[24] It will prevent them from straying

---

[23] Revelation 9:20-21; 21:8, 27; 22:15

[24] "You were taught, with regard to your former way of life, to put off your old self, which is being corrupted by its deceitful desires; [23] to be made new in the attitude of your minds; [24] and to put on the new self, created to be like God in true righteousness and holiness." Ephesians 4:22-24

away from us through eternity. Man's moral nature helps them discern between right and wrong, fair and inequitable. Unredeemed man thinks they can live by their own rules, so they disdain our moral laws[25] and mistakenly think I will allow them to enter heaven. Continuing in their sin prevents them from being reconciled with us and holds them in their state of condemnation. That crushes me inside because I sacrificed so much for them so they could escape their eternal ruin.[26] When one truly becomes my child, the desire to develop their morality becomes evident through their actions."

Beauty

"As you look around, you will notice the beauty I prominently displayed throughout this world in countless ways. It is not an accident that you see so much beauty on earth. We love beauty and intentionally placed it everywhere on planet earth. We designed the earth to be a pleasant place. Often we make some beauty temporary. Such as a sunset or flowers that bloom in just a short time. The brief displays allow you to look for or anticipate other displays of beauty in other places.

"You see my imaginative design in a sunset, an autumn display of colorful trees, water, mountains, and waterfalls, and a myriad of other scenes of splendor. The beauty of this earth is my gift to humankind for them to enjoy. The image of God allows humanity to both appreciate and express beauty. Artists delight in communicating splendor in their paintings or carvings. Poets, composers, and singers present beautiful worship songs as they declare such things as who I am, how great is my faithfulness and love, and their experiences with me. Such themes honor me, for

---

[25] "They are darkened in their understanding and separated from the life of God because of the ignorance that is in them due to the hardening of their hearts. Having lost all sensitivity, they have given themselves over to sensuality so as to indulge in every kind of impurity, and they are full of greed." Ephesians 4:18-19

[26] "For God so loved the world that he gave his one and only Son, that whoever believes in him shall not perish but have eternal life." John 3:16. See also Romans 5:6-8.

35

they express our image in their creativity. Even though not all musicians are reconciled to me, they still possess the ability to present beautiful music through their instruments and voices. They can be creative because our image is part of their being. Here is another essential truth you need to consider about beauty. Why is a man drawn to the beauty of a woman? Her beauty attracts him to her so they can develop a meaningful relationship built on mutual love, interests, and commitment. This leads us to our next point."

Relationships

"We think that the most exciting part of humanity having our image is their ability to establish, enjoy, and engage in relationships. When you think about it, relationships define life. Those who don't know how to develop relationships are empty. That's why confused people look to things like money, popularity, power, prestige, drugs, alcohol, and various pleasures to fill that emptiness in their souls. They miss the realization that it is in relationships that humanity reaches their potential and finds their greatest joy.

"Marriage, when done right, is an illustration of the intimacy of the relationship we want you to experience with us. When the man and woman were in the garden, they were both naked. That is a declaration of more than physical nakedness. They were able to be fully transparent in their relationship with each other. Even now, when they enjoy physical intimacy, it allows them to open up more fully and with greater freedom. It is this same transparency and openness that we want you to experience with us. Marriage offers a picture of the honesty and openness in a relationship that we want you to enjoy with us. It's one of the great expressions of unity, devotion, and love that leads to a deeper discovery of each other."

"Jesus, I can't get over how you value us so highly. You chose to go through all that pain of dying on the cross to re-establish a relationship with us so we could have an intimate fellowship with you. It must hurt you to see that even Christians don't value this relationship as they should. They look at salvation as a list of rules and responsibilities rather than a relationship with you. Legalism thrives because people want someone to tell them what to do rather than learn how to be in a vibrant relationship with the Spirit to guide them. They seek to steal the Holy Spirit's relationship with the believer so they can lord their authority over their followers. Others use beautiful worship and music expressions that lack the heart to gain your favor and declare their devotion to you. That expression of worship without heart is certainly an insult to you."

"Jim, you are our creation. We have set our love on humanity. Just as a parent enjoys watching their children grow, learn, and come to appreciate a relationship with them on an ever-deepening level, so we too enjoy that with humanity.'

'We look forward to them entering into a meaningful relationship with us, and the deeper it goes, the more they will find they love us. I delight when my children learn to develop meaningful relationships with us. We sought to use terms about salvation that indicate they are entering a relationship with us. We talk about such things as love, kindness, grace, and goodness. We make each believer our child, deed them their own home in heaven, make them citizens, give them a shared inheritance with Christ, they become our friends, and we allow them to reign with us.[27]"

"Now, let me get back to what I was saying because this is exciting. When we talk about the marriage relationship between a man and a woman, we want them to enjoy and value it because they understand the relationship we desire with them. In the Old Testament, my Father called Israel, His wife,[28] and as you know, in

---

[27] **Love** – John 3:16, Romans 5:6-8,8:38-39, Ephesians 2:4, 5:2, 1 John 4:9-10. **Kindness** - Titus 3:4. **Grace** – Romans 3:24, 5:2, 15, 16:24, 2 Corinthians 6:1. **Goodness** – 2 Thessalonians 1:11. Made us a **child of God** – John 1:12, Romans 8:16,1 John 3:2, **Home in heaven** – John 14:2-3, 2, Corinthians 5:8. **Shared inheritance** - Romans 8:17. **Citizen of heaven** – Philippians 3:20, Ephesians 2:19. **You become Our friends** – John 15:14-15. **Reign with Christ** – Revelation 20:6, 22:5.

[28] "I gave faithless Israel her certificate of divorce and sent her away because of all her adulteries. Yet I saw that her unfaithful sister Judah had no fear; she also went out and committed adultery." Jeremiah 3:8. The fact that God divorced Israel is indication that He looked on her as His wife. The book of Hosea tells of God accepting Israel back.

the New Testament, the church is the bride of Christ.[29] We are serious about being in an ongoing and intimate relationship with humanity.

"That depth of relationship we seek with you was expressed by me when I spoke to the Father about you in my high priestly prayer that John faithfully recorded in John 17. I'm so glad John documented that because I definitely expressed my heart for you. These two truths help you understand why the image of God in you is so important. It gives you the basics of a relationship with the Trinity.

"Do you know the two requests that I value, Jim?"

"I sure do, Jesus. The first one was in verse 3 when you defined the real essence of eternal life. *Now, this is eternal life: that they know you, the only true God, and Jesus Christ, whom you have sent.* (John 17:3) So being possessors of the image of God allows us to have fellowship with you. One of the benefits is expressing all our thoughts to you. You will, in turn, share who you are, reveal what you are like, and give us your power."

"Jim, that is right. We want to share our life with you, and the good thing is that no one has to wait until they arrive in heaven. In salvation, my children can experience an intimate fellowship with us now. It pains us that not all of our children choose to do so.

"The other one is found later in the chapter where I talk to my Father about the unity I want you to experience with each other and with us. I requested that you may experience the very same unity that the Father and I have. We embrace you fully into our relationship Jim. Now read about that in 17:20-23 for me."

---

[29] "I am jealous for you with a godly jealousy. I promised you to one husband, to Christ, so that I might present you as a pure virgin to him." 2 Corinthians 11:2 "Hallelujah! For our Lord God Almighty reigns. [7] Let us rejoice and be glad and give him glory! For the wedding of the Lamb has come, and his bride has made herself ready. Revelation 19 7

"Ok, I'll be glad to." "*My prayer is not for them alone. I also pray for those who will believe in me through their message, that all of them may be one, Father, just as you are in me, and I am in you. May they also be in us so that the world may believe that you have sent me. I have given them the glory that you gave me, that they may be one as we are one—I in them and you in me—so that they may be brought to complete unity. Then the world will know that you sent me and have loved them even as you have loved me.*"[30] Jesus, you sure are offering us something special by asking the Father to experience the same unity that you have with each other. You aren't holding anything back from us. By that, you are inviting us into your inner circle, aren't you?"

"We are unwavering Jim about fully accepting humanity. We want everyone to enjoy all that we have prepared for them. We are disappointed when people don't take our provision seriously, but we have given them free will to make that choice.

"Because our nature is in you, you are fully equipped to have fellowship, not just with one another, but with us as well.[31] Fellowship tops the list of all the qualities included in the divine image. Eternity will be special because of our abundant opportunities to enter into regular fellowship. Never will we tire of each other or get bored because we run out of things to discuss. Our conversations will always be stimulating and fulfilling. You will always take something away from these times that will cause you to think about our exciting times together. Anticipating the next encounter will be the norm through eternity. The more you get to know us, the greater your ability will become to express meaningful and creative praise. You entered a living relationship in your reconciliation with us. That will guide and enrich your life forever."

---

[30] John 17:20–23

[31] 1 John 1:3–4 (NIV) "*We proclaim to you what we have seen and heard, so that you also may have fellowship with us. And our fellowship is with the Father and with his Son, Jesus Christ. ⁴ We write this to make our joy complete.*"

Not all make it

"Lord Jesus, there are many who have rejected you, so they won't be going to heaven. How will that affect them? Does the image of God leave them when they die, or will it continue to have some lasting effect on them?"

With sadness in His eyes, Jesus responded: "They never lose our image. It is our image that makes them human. Now you understand why humanity is so valuable. When they die, they will understand just how ingrained our image is in them. A significant portion of their suffering in hell will be that they will have a longing to be able to express that part of their nature. Still, they will never have access to the empowerment of the Holy Spirit to experience it. They will cry out for the ability to express our image, for it will continually crave fulfillment. Their rejection of reconciliation holds them captive to their ruined condition, thus preventing them from ever expressing the image we placed in them. That will have a massive effect on causing them to have a distinct kind of suffering in hell. No matter how much they yearn to experience living out our image, they will lack that ability, even more so in hell than on earth in their unredeemed state. That desire to express the image of God will always burn in their soul with no fulfillment possible. It will become increasingly important to them as they realize they can never experience the life their heart desires with God.

"The way people can express fullness in the development of our image is through the Holy Spirit's ministry. When I came to earth, I laid aside the independent use of my attributes[32] as God and then lived in complete dependence on the Spirit. Through His enablement, guidance, and wisdom, I did all my teaching, miracles, and works of power. The redeemed, who allow the Spirit to work in their life now, can express our image effectually in their lives

---

[32] "In your relationships with one another, have the same mindset as Christ Jesus: Who, being in very nature God, did not consider equality with God something to be used to his own advantage" Philippians 2:5-6

and maintain a relationship with us. These are the main features of heaven we want you to enjoy with us. My friend, we have many good things planned for you beyond your wildest imagination. That is what makes us sad when people willfully reject reconciliation with us and seal their eternal fate in hell.

"In a similar vein of thought, the Spirit gifts all of my children. These spiritual gifts allow them to use their talents and abilities to build up other believers and carry out our eternal plans. The Holy Spirit empowers your talents and abilities to help you use them for our purposes that have infinite worth. It's not enough to have skills and abilities, but they must have our enablement and direction to make their use count for eternity. (See Romans 12:3-8; 1 Corinthians 12)

The purpose of our gifts, talents, and abilities

"That brings me to the culmination of what I have to say. All the gifts, talents, abilities, creativity, interests, and characteristics that comprise the image of God in you, along with your ability to engage in relationships, will typify the activities and motivation of your life in heaven. These qualities in the divine image will give you creative ways to live and explore your creativity and thus continue to open your understanding of God in a wide variety of ways. When you use your gifts, talents, abilities, and interests, they are not an end in themselves but a means of gaining a practical understanding of God so you can, throughout eternity, bring your praise and adoration to God in fresh, creative ways. We gave you all of these abilities to open your understanding of God so you can delight in us and better honor, serve and worship your Creator."

Jim could not hold back: "This is a neat concept I hadn't considered before. *The way you made us is not just for our earthly lives but is a preview for how we will function, and see life in heaven.* Wow! I can see why some people will have tears[33] for a

---

[33] "He will wipe every tear from their eyes. There will be no more death' ᵘ or mourning or

41

while when they get to heaven. They will realize that they did not take seriously the way you made them, and they came empty-handed, despite all the ways you equipped them to learn and serve."

"That's correct, Jim. It pains me that so many don't value the gifts, talents, abilities, and creativity that we endowed them. Some admire the way we endowed others but discount the worth of their personality and their gifts, talents, and abilities. That is a glaring insult against the Holy Spirit, for they are saying that He didn't know what He was doing when He placed these gifts, talents, and abilities in them."

With a melancholy response, I said, "I know I've been guilty of that many times over the years. I do apologize for not valuing what the Spirit gave me, as well as what He did for me. I did not always honor the way you made me."

"You have already been forgiven, Jim. With that, I think it is time for you to wake from your sleep. You will enjoy the plans we have for you in how you will grow in your ability as you and Lorrie finish your lives. We have some special plans for you when you are finally home with us. Knowing how you get so excited about things, we know you will not contain yourself in what we plan. Your joy will be FULL."

With that, I heard the dogs barking. They seemed anxious to go outside because they knew that food would be waiting for them when they came in. I dressed so I could let them out. However, my mind could not let go of the fantastic time I had just spent with Jesus. I thought about many of the things He said, for I wanted to write them down as quickly as possible. However, what captivated me most was how delightful the time was with Him. I felt so comfortable and at ease

---

crying or pain, for the old order of things has passed away." Revelation 21:4 -- Some will argue with me on this point. I think there is room for tears at the judgment seat of believers. Many have squandered their lives, and there will be regret. However, afterwards, they will not have to look back at their failures in which they dishonored the Lord. Jesus fully accepts them based on His finished work on the cross.

in His presence. He treated me with a love that let me know I was unique to Him. I shall never forget how heartbroken He was when He spoke of those who rejected Him and thus chose to remain separated eternally from Him.

My thoughts easily stayed focused on my encounter with Jesus. By far, the dominating thought that would not go away is that I longed to be back in His presence. That's coming, but I will serve Him faithfully and talk to others about my great friend Jesus until then.

The Image of God

It is in this teaching that we learn why each person is indispensable. God created all humanity in His image. Comprehending this truth recognizes who we are, why we are here, and the purpose of life. It is the reason worldwide evangelism is so important. Such knowledge is fundamental in determining the direction of our lives and stabilizing the purpose of our existence. The reality of this teaching also applies to eternity.

It is my premise in this book that heaven will be the continued opportunity to understand and express the image of God in the way we live. That image will continue to develop as we learn what God is like and how that understanding will continue to transform us to become more like Jesus Christ. Because God created us in His image, I make my case for what our daily life will be like in heaven.

God's image motivates our intellect, emotions, and will. This image gives us the qualities and characteristics of God. Appropriately expressing this image requires us to make certain lifestyle choices. God calls us to be holy, show love, and value others as we walk in the Spirit.[34] God's image allows us to be creative, to have a personal and intimate relationship with God and man, value people, and get along with them.

---

34 Romans 12, Ephesians 4:22-32, Colossians 3

We will find pleasure in beauty, work, and being productive. We will recognize the dignity of every person because of the way God made each of us. We are rational and self-conscious because God's image is in us all, but only His children, those reconciled to Him, will be able to continue to express it.

Our ability to communicate details, ideas, theories, emotions, and instructions comes from the image of God. The divine nature equips us with a moral conscience, the emotive ability to love and enjoy life, and to have self-determination, that is, the free will to make choices and act responsibly. Seen also is a personality that is different in each nature and will continue to develop in that unique way through eternity. Why should these qualities of our personality, interests, and abilities not follow us into eternity? Let us always value the way God made us and figure out how He wants to use our particular personality in this life to live and serve for His glory.

God's image in each human equips us to appreciate beauty in a million different ways and find untold expression in life. Art, music, gardening, and writings are expressions of beauty that help articulate our admiration of God.

Finally, God's image means that we are moral beings responsible for our actions. No human will ever cease to exist. Death moves them into a different realm. Why then would anyone not take seriously their opportunity to prepare for eternity? Deception comes when people accept non-biblical viewpoints. I refer to such ideas as the teachings that say there is no life after death, continual reincarnation after death, or some second chance after death. Following death, each person faces God's judgment of their life.[35] God has only two eternal destinations available from which to choose.[36] An old gospel song says, "Life has many choices; eternity has only two." Choosing reconciliation takes

---

35 "Just as people are destined to die once, and after that to face judgment." Hebrews 9:27
36 "Then he will say to those on his left, 'Depart from me, you who are cursed, into the eternal fire prepared for the devil and his angels." "Then they will go away to eternal punishment, but the righteous to eternal life." Matthew 25:41a, 46

one to heaven. To reject reconciliation with God causes one to remain His enemy through eternity.

In the rest of this book, I seek to show how expressing the image of God can be the factor that motivates our actions and directs the way we will live in heaven and relate to God.

Another Facet of the Image

After I published this book, my former church invited me to preach. I decided to speak on the topic of heaven. I laid the foundation of my message by talking about the image of God. In preparation for this message, I discovered a verse that needed consideration with this topic. In **Isaiah 44:2,** it says, *"This is what the LORD says he who made you, who formed you in the womb"* The word *formed* is the same word used to speak of a **potter** *shaping clay* or a **woodcarver** *creating an image*. This term can indicate developing any artistic creation. Contemplate with me the creativity of a truly imaginative person. They never make duplicates of their paintings. Each one is unique. God is a creative artist. It, therefore, makes sense that this talented creator forms each person differently as He fashions them in the womb.[37] It's easy to notice that everyone looks different. The uniqueness doesn't stop there. Every person has a unique purpose and a distinctive set of talents, interests, and abilities to use in life. As I thought about these differences, an idea struck me. God placed different portions of his image in each of us to relate to Him uniquely.

Let me give you a personal illustration of how this may play out in God's plans. My wife and I had two daughters. Interestingly, our youngest daughter thinks and acts a lot like me, and our oldest daughter responds to life, much like her mother. My youngest and I see life in a

---

[37] Psalm 139:13-17 "For you formed my inmost being. You knit me together in my mother's womb. I will give thanks to you, for I am fearfully and wonderfully made. Your works are wonderful. My soul knows that very well. My frame wasn't hidden from you, when I was made in secret, woven together in the depths of the earth. Your eyes saw my body. In your book they were all written, the days that were ordained for me, when as yet there were none of them." (NHEB)

very similar way. We both have a heart for people and are outgoing in our passion for the things of God. We don't have to explain why we do or say something because we understand each other. Our sense of humor is similar. We are both sensitive to the needs of others and desire to help people right away. My oldest daughter looks at life so much like her mother. They are both very organized and deep thinkers. Whereas Heidi and I are outgoing, they are introverts. Nancy and Heather understand each other when they look with disgust at people who do foolish things. My oldest daughter doesn't appreciate or get my jokes like my youngest daughter. My youngest daughter and I like to say and write what we feel. Nancy and Heather think that everything needs to be grammatically correct. They helped me become more accurate in my writing skills over the years.

God painted each of us with various hues of His temperaments, abilities, passions, and gifts so we can relate to our heavenly Father differently. In using these expressions of our personality, we uniquely relate to God and understand Him in our inimitable way. We notice something about God that others don't always get or easily see. We comprehend God with a different perspective, which draws us to search out more about that feature of God. That becomes our impetus to learn more and dig deeper to understand God from our distinctive perspective. These passions will drive us to understand God more fully. Each of us will 'get' God from our exclusive perspective because of our unique understanding of a particular aspect of Him.

Try to understand this teaching by relating it to the kinds of Christians in various churches. Some love more in-depth Bible teaching and enjoy going into the complexity of its meaning. They like observing the meaning of words, studying the historical context, and pulling scriptures together to give the text fuller meaning. They love learning about God through the study of God's word.

Other Christians are interested in experiencing God and His power. Yes, God can heal because He is all-powerful and has given us His Spirit. They are not afraid to claim His power in prayer and trust God for the impossible.

Christians love variety in their music. Some enjoy the old hymns, and others like contemporary worship styles. Some want no musical accompaniment, and others use instruments. Some sing with little emotion, and others are full of passion and put their hearts into it. Can we accept them the way they are and recognize that is their way of relating to God? If God placed that interest in them, who are we really rejecting when we are critical of them?

Christians involve themselves in the church through various types of service, and as a result, they serve, help, build up, bring to the Lord, and love others. One church of believers is not better than any other church; they are just different and accomplish a unique purpose in learning about God, serving Him, worshiping Him, and expressing their faith.

It is a problem when believers think that their way of doing church is *the* right way and forget that God has saved and gifted every Christian and given them various interests, passions, gifts, and abilities. Therefore, they have the freedom to express themselves differently because they relate to God with the unique skills He gave them. God planned it that way. The leaders who want uniformity in the way people need to act and serve God fail to see God's variety in His people. What do you think their response will be when they see these unique personality expressions continue to manifest in heaven?

Understanding the different aspects of God's image placed in His people is a significant truth to recognize. God made each of us unique, which helps us appreciate our differences and value the uniqueness of others. We are all important, for our differences will draw us close to God in diverse ways. God gave us these differences for a purpose, so there is no reason to scorn who we are or how God made us. Many think God shortchanged them because they are not like those they admire. They see the gold in the personality of others but fail to see the riches God has placed in them.

Have you ever noticed the various kinds of friendships you have? There is Justin, who values his co-workers. Grahame is the one you go to with your problems. He always seems to figure out the right solution

47

to your problem. Chris is the friend you enjoy talking to about sports, but he is also your hunting buddy. Jeremiah is the guy you can talk to about computers, the latest games, and stimulating websites to help you stay up on the best ideas for work. Angus is the man you confide in because he enables you to tackle spiritual concerns. He always has an answer that offers you great insight when deciding. If we are fortunate, we have various friends that relate to us on different levels. Each friend helps you enjoy or deal with a separate area of life.

We find that we need a variety of people to meet the various needs in facing life, enjoying life, and navigating the difficulties and the unknowns of life. Each relates to us differently. That is a picture of our relationship with God. He doesn't need us to meet His needs, but He wants us to understand Him uniquely. He placed our various interests and abilities in us to relate to different aspects of His being. God designed people with these diverse interests and skills to understand Him and relate to Him in the innumerable facets of His nature. They will never tire of exploring *the unsearchable depths of His being throughout eternity.*

"He does great things past finding out; yes, marvelous things without number." (Job 9:10)

"Great is the LORD and greatly to be praised, and His greatness is unsearchable." (Psalm 145:3)

"Oh, the depth of the riches both of the wisdom and the knowledge of God! How unsearchable are his judgments, and his ways past tracing out!" (Ro 11:33)

As we develop our relationship with God, our desire, shaped by the uniqueness of our makeup, will draw us to seek a better understanding of God and those extra-ordinary aspects of His glory. Some may concentrate on one aspect of God's creation, such as animals, plants, or the stars. Others may focus on worship, singing, art, or writing to express God's greatness. Just as we relate to people differently, God designed each of us to seek out a different aspect of His glory to focus on so that we can further our understanding of Him. Knowing this truth will prepare us to develop our relationship with God and worship Him with greater understanding and appreciation because it will come out of our unique attraction to Him.

The next time you find yourself judging other Christians in how they look at God or the way they worship or serve Him, take time to think about how they may be expressing their ability to see or express the uniqueness of God's image in a particular way. Just because people worship God differently than you do, or emphasize a different aspect of God than you, doesn't make them wrong, only different. Learn to recognize God's unique image in each believer.

The next time you feel sorry for yourself by thinking you are insignificant, it is time to remember that God created you in His image. That means He made you exactly as He wanted, that is, in a unique way so you can understand Him in a different way than others. God made you for that purpose, which gives your life richness of meaning and significance. Understanding this truth makes this life and the next very exciting, as we shall see in the rest of this book.

I trust you are now ready to explore the possibilities of what God has in store for us when we get to heaven. I want you to look forward to heaven with greater anticipation because of the kinds of good things you can more realistically anticipate.

* * * * * * * * *

> It is my premise in this book that heaven will offer the continued opportunity to understand and express the image of God in us. As we use this ability it will help us see God in His greatness and will, in turn, be the basis of our praise and adoration.

Therefore, "they are before the throne of God
and serve him day and night in his temple;
and he who sits on the throne
will shelter them with his presence.
'Never again will they hunger,
never again will they thirst.
The sun will not beat down on them,'
nor any scorching heat.
For the Lamb at the center of the throne
will be their shepherd;
'he will lead them to springs of living water.'
'And God will wipe away every tear from their eyes.'"

Revelation 7:15–17 (NIV)

* * * * * * * * * * * *

"If the Lord should bring a wicked man to heaven, heaven would be hell to him, for he who loves not grace upon earth will never love it in heaven."

Chapter Three -- Nancy's Angel Escort

WHEN NANCY DIED, all I saw was her taking her last breath. Her body went quiet. Her struggle was over. Her body was the house she dwelt in for 68 years. God refitted her with a new body after leaving the hospital that night. I didn't see any of this transpire, but it happened.

Just as the account of the rich man and Lazarus recorded in Luke 16, an angel came to greet Nancy and escort her to her new home. The angel told me his name was Asriel. God chose him to be with Nancy because Asriel likes to laugh and has a good sense of humor, which Nancy always enjoyed. Many angels are by the book and take their people directly to heaven. Asriel has a sense of adventure. He took a few side trips along the way to show Nancy some interesting sights. On their journey, he also stopped and invited her to sit so they could talk about life in heaven. Nancy always liked to know what was going to happen, so I think that is why God sent this particular angel to greet her. He wants to make sure his people are informed and have some fun along the way.

Often when our saved loved one dies, we are sad and don't think about the joy they are experiencing with their new freedom and the joy that comes as they anticipate entering the presence of the Lord soon. Our pain and sorrow from the human side cloud our vision of the unseen world they enter. They recognize that their purpose on earth was to prepare for heaven and be with God.

Nancy struggled with arthritis for much of her life. The pain was challenging, and it often sapped her energy so she could not enter the family's activities. Now her body was pain-free.[38] The sluggishness of

---

[38] "He will wipe every tear from their eyes. There will be no more death, or mourning or crying

the old body was gone, and she was experiencing new energy. Her freedom from pain was so welcome. She didn't realize she could feel so good. *"This new body is great."*[39] That was not all that changed. There was a new freedom in her spirit. As Nancy tried to identify what was so different about her feelings, she realized she had no more fear, depression, or negative thoughts. There were no more nagging temptations from her sinful nature and no enticements to focus on self. Gone were her inward struggles with sin within. It is tremendous that all effects of sin were purged from every part of her being. Never again would she feel her sinful nature's influence. Nothing negative would cause her to struggle, just peace and a constant sense of well-being. She was getting used to this new life rather quickly, and **she liked it**.

As she traveled with Asriel, her understanding started to comprehend things she could never figure out before. Her mind was exploding with new knowledge. Suddenly she realized her eyeglasses were missing. Her eyesight was clear, and the richness of color was more intense, which added to the beauty she was beholding.

Asriel talked about many details of heaven. He shared what other humans said about experiencing God's presence for the first time. Nancy was getting more eager to be there. Her heart could hardly contain the anticipation she felt, and she broke into song. Nancy loved to sing on earth and was now pleasantly surprised by her new pipes for singing. Never before did she have such a range and clarity of voice. Her heart was so full that her voice burst into praise to God.

Asriel smiled as he took it all in. "I never get tired of watching people respond to their new body and life, especially as they start to experience their freedom and more fully comprehend what God has done to them. Everyone that breaks into singing always uses a new song to proclaim God's glory, and I get to hear it. It doesn't get much better than this. God has given me the best job ever!"

---

or pain, for the old order of things has passed away" Revelation 21:4

39 1 Corinthians 15:51-53 - This passage not only talks about the rapture of the church, but also the time when we will receive our new body.

"Asriel, on earth, I experienced great times with God through my Bible study and seeing how God worked in my life as well as in others, but then it faded after a while. Will that happen to us in heaven also? Will the initial excitement become a distant memory that we will only pursue in heaven?"

"Oh no, Nancy, heaven will be a place where you will never tire of learning about God and seeing His greatness. God will never disappoint you. You will join with people as they express their praise to God and shout with joy the acclamation of what they have learned about God. Things will never get old, but then again, we will never stop learning. Every day will be a fresh experience with God that will continue to excite your soul. Just as friends inspire you in specific ways in your walk with God and the use of your abilities, so you will find that every person in heaven will build something different and positive into your life. As they learn more about God, they will always be eager to share that as well."

"Will there only be large group praise sessions, such as are depicted in the book of Revelation, or will we sing solos and gather in small groups to praise? Will we be able to hold personal praise gatherings to honor Lord Jesus?"

With a twinkle in his eye, Asriel said, "Yes, Nancy."

"Did you learn that from my husband? He always responded that way to Ron, a friend from our first pastorate."

"I know some about your husband as well as Ron. Let me remind you that we angels don't know everything. Like you, we have a lot to learn about God and the individuals we meet. What I do know is that one of the reasons God sent me to you was because He knew you would be acquainted with my sense of humor. By the way, my answer is correct. We will have some corporate praise, and then groups will gather to worship God all around heaven. Individuals will sing freely by themselves and with a few friends. Singing is a way God gifted humans to express praise and adoration of Him."

Nancy never felt hurried when she was with Asriel. He answered her questions about life in heaven. She could tell that Asriel showed her the honor God has for each of His saints.

"Well, Nancy, we are about there. When you arrive at the gates, your mom and Jim's dad will welcome you. You will then meet your relatives and friends who arrived before you. Take your time to catch up with them. After all, you do have all eternity. When you finish at the meet and greet reception, you will have some time to yourself to look around heaven, and then Jesus wants to meet with you and answer all those questions you have."

"Asriel, you made my journey to heaven most pleasant. Thank you for your kindness. Will I see you around?

"Of course," he said happily. "I'll be around off and on until after the end of the Kingdom Age. My Ubering of people up here keeps me busy, but I'll look for you. When Jim dies, the Lord said I could get him too. I'll be sure to tell him all about what's happening with you. So Nancy, are you ready to meet everyone and get started on the life you had anticipated since you got saved back when you were six years old at Fenton Bible Church?"

"Thank you again, Asriel. I am ready and eager to get started. Things have disappointed me at times, but I know there will be no disappointments here. Goodbye, my friend."

As quickly as Asriel appeared to her, he was gone. He's off to escort another believer to heaven, no doubt. She thought, perhaps, he will use some of those same jokes on them as he used on me. As Nancy turned and headed into the newcomer's reception hall, there was an anticipation of excitement. Who would be there to welcome her home? Before she entered, she stopped for just a moment for one last thought: *"One thing for certain is that I will have nothing to fear here, ever again."*

"Let's get this show on the road," she spoke aloud as she grabbed the door handle to enter. With the greatest of anticipations in her heart and a smile on her face, she declared, "I'm finally going to meet God!"

Chapter Four -- Meeting with Jesus

WHEN NANCY STEPPED INTO THE GREETING ROOM, her family and friends, who arrived home first, greeted her. The reunion was sweet, and there was no pressure to end their fellowship time. Meeting those with whom she had established earthly relationships made heaven feel homier. The fellowship just seemed to pick up where it left off on earth. To her amazement, she discovered that the residents didn't know what was happening back on earth with family and friends, except when one in their circle arrived and filled them in on all that transpired.

After the excitement of meeting her mom, Jim's dad, Uncle Floyd, and other relatives and friends, Nancy could have some personal time. Many changes in the horizon would require adjustments. What can she do in her new body, and how would she view life differently? No longer would she be plagued with sin, doubt, fear, or hurt from others. She noticed that some signs of her introverted lifestyle didn't disappear entirely. She liked her alone time to think and process everything. That wasn't such a bad trait because there are no time schedules in heaven.

Nancy took her time to stroll through heaven and become acclimated and acquainted with people. As she walked through the streets, she noticed the calmness and peace of heart that seemed to envelop her whole being. She didn't remember experiencing such tranquility, even though sometimes on earth seemed to come close. The atmosphere of the entire place felt like it was exuding God's love. His love was so tangible as if she could breathe it in. God's love seemed to cradle her soul and make her feel complete and accepted. How could anyone fear in this atmosphere?[40] God certainly knows how to make us feel at home and welcome!

---

[40] "There is no fear in love. But perfect love drives out fear, because fear has to do with punishment. The one who fears is not made perfect in love. 1 John 4:18

55

Nancy lost track of time as she walked heaven's streets. She observed the groups of saints gathered to worship and praise God with their instruments and singing. She smiled as she heard various guitar players. Guitars were prevalent all over heaven. To her surprise, some of the songs she heard were familiar ones she knew back on earth. Then it dawned on her, "Well, I suppose if God inspired them for the earth, they would be just as appropriate in heaven too." She took the time to listen and found that she could quickly pick up the words to new songs, and the tunes were so inviting they lured her in to sing along.

"I can't believe how incredible my memory has been since I got here. I'm able to remember everything in vivid detail. It just seems so natural to recall words to songs, details of conversations, and especially everyone's name."

She remarked to herself how she recognized the more profound meaning and implications of the message of each song with complete clarity. I sure look forward to how God will continue to open my understanding about Him and life in the eons to come.

Some of the groups she passed had several instrumental accompaniments; others had such good harmony that they didn't need any. Their close harmony enthralled her. Some groups sounded like one voice. It was like nothing she had ever heard. When worshiping, many of the songs had counter melodies. She could distinguish each one and loved the way it enhanced the praise. On earth, many choirs had a few good voices that carried the rest who could not sing very well, but here in heaven, everyone could carry their part and knew how to sing. Her love for music did not subside in heaven; in fact, it was much more intense and that she loved.

Nancy allowed herself the time to process the new intense feelings. As she contemplated the various aspects of heaven, there was almost a giddiness stirring in her. It thrilled her not only to be in heaven but also to have this satisfying, intimate relationship with God. "*What is that feeling?*" she asked herself. The Holy Spirit let her chew on it for a while, and then recognition started to dawn. I know what it is. It's JOY! "I have never experienced such uninhibited joy before." "Holy Spirit, is that from you?" She knew it was, without Him having to say anymore. In the days ahead, she discovered that the fruit of the Spirit had a more robust expression in the way she experienced life and relationships. As she would develop the fruit of the Spirit, she was getting to know how God expresses Himself to us. She loved how this understanding colored how she saw things and enhanced her dealings with people. The Holy Spirit taught her that this would be a growing experience all through eternity as she lived out her unique expression of the richness of the image of God.

She longed to hear the Lord in response to her prayers and conversations on earth. Oh, how many times did she cry out and ask for help with her depression and struggles with sickness and pain, but she didn't hear a response from God. That was not the case anymore in heaven. Ever since she arrived, the Lord responded to each inquiry and her worship. It was no longer, what seemed like a one-sided conversation of faith, but a daily reality with the God she loved and enjoyed. Nancy liked this method of fellowship with her Savior. "*This won't grow old for me,*" she said with a bit of giggle and an enormous smile on her face.

There was nothing dull or mundane about life. It seemed like there were always new things to experience and enjoy. She not only had long talks and walks with her friends but spent time with those well-known saints she'd read about in the Bible and knew about in history. Nancy thought it might be hard to meet these people, or they might not be interested in talking to her about their life. She was pleasantly surprised to find that each one was easy to approach and took joy in telling her their story of how God dealt with them and used them during their life. Each one shared their feelings as they reflected on God's mission for them and their accompanying struggles, fears, and concerns. None put on airs of being better than others as they freely shared their story. She sensed a true spirit of humility, knowing that all that happened was to honor God and carry out His will. While talking with each one, she understood why God chose them for their particular task. "*How wise God is in the way He understands who people are and what they can do.*"

I met Jesus

Nancy can still remember the first time she met with Jesus, clear as day. When she saw Him, her heart skipped a beat or two. She was in awe of Him, and instead of bowing down to worship, as she thought she would, she ran over and gave him a great big hug, and He returned the embrace. He then told her of His love for her. "I'm so glad you are here. I've been anticipating you and wanted us to meet face to face."

Her meeting with Him was unhurried. He talked with her at length. She felt comfortable to be herself in His presence — what a delightful conversation they had. One of His reasons for the meeting was to share ways He and the Spirit worked in her life through the years. He spoke explicitly about the incidents. He also talked about how He and the Spirit used Nancy to accomplish their will and influence others in their faith-walk. Jesus helped her recognize just how important she was to Him as she faithfully served Him. As Jesus spoke, everything became clear and evident about how God used her life to accomplish His will. She had no idea how closely the Spirit was working in her life. The indiscernible workings of God blended seamlessly into her thinking and actions.

Something else made an indelible impression on Nancy when she met with Him. It was His love for her. Being in His presence made her feel secure. She could never question His love for her anymore. She drank in every word while He shared His heart about how He delighted in her service, love, and worship. His hands grabbed her attention when she looked fully upon Him. It was his nail-scarred hands. He still carried those scars in heaven! As she scrutinized His hands, her mind was consumed with a new understanding of the suffering she caused Him when He died on the cross for her sins. His death and suffering provided acceptance into His family and gave her a home she was now enjoying in heaven. Many other truths engulfed her mind, but she was just glad she was here in Jesus' presence. His total acceptance brought an indescribable peace over her entire being.

Time is very different in heaven, so she had no idea how long their meeting was. It seemed like it was long, yet there was no sense of hurry or urgency. Jesus truly loved her and valued their relationship. They both enjoyed being together and talking. When Nancy felt it was time to leave, Jesus spoke a word of encouragement.

"Nancy, before you go on your way, I want you to know that you can come back and visit me anytime. I will always have time for you. We are all friends and family, so don't ever hesitate, even if you just want to shoot the breeze and hang out over coffee and pie together. You know the tree of life has a different fruit each month, so pie choices are always changing. Please realize that I will always welcome you to spend time with me."

Two thoughts struck her. The first was that Jesus called her by name, just as an old friend would speak her name with familiarity. The second was that His invitation to hang out with Him delighted her. Often people say those things, but Jesus is truth, so she recognized that such a statement was not a hollow invitation. Her smile was full and genuine. She anticipated that many things in heaven would bring a smile to her face. That is such a good part of heaven.

Jesus hadn't finished and continued His parting words. "Nancy, I know how you struggled with inferiority a lot during your life, so never forget that you are special to me. My death, for you, was no small thing. It was a declaration that you are important and that I truly love and value you. Nothing can change that."

"I also want you to know that in the future, we have some exciting plans for you. These plans include sharing your life with a group of people for a special project in which we want you to participate. The first purpose is to seek ways to honor you for what you did for me with your life. The second is to help you understand how the Holy Spirit and I worked in your life over the years. We protected you, guided you, and developed you and your abilities all through life. Finally, I want you to see how you fit into my big picture of what I accomplished on earth. That will also involve the people who had affected your life with their influence, even before your life began. I know you will be delighted to take part in this project. Make sure you have fun, and enjoy sharing your story. I'm going to show you how history, actually my story has a grand theme that I carried out fully, and you were part of it."

Nancy giggled a little and then replied, "I'm interested in how you will show that to me. I think you will be showing me, I mean all of us, many things that will truly delight us as eternity rolls on. Lord Jesus, life here is about honoring you; I don't understand why you even take the time to honor me in this way. I'm not complaining, mind you, so thank you."

"I understand that Nancy, but I want you to appreciate that your life has honored me. It was not just your life alone, but also the others with whom you worked. I want all the residents of heaven to know how everything and everyone fit together and how I worked out the good in your life. Some of my children will stop by to interview you in a short time. They will use the creativity that the Spirit has endowed them with to feature your life in artistic ways. Until then, continue to get used to heaven and feel comfortable here. After all, Jesus said with a twinkle in His eye; you are *finally home*."[41]

Nancy caught the inference of what He said, but that just added to the warmth she felt in her soul for Him. Her mind started to swim with all of what Jesus told her. All she could focus on was wondering what Jesus meant by honoring her. Then she said to herself, "Well, if Jesus planned it, then it would be good, and I'm not going to fret about it." She was willing to wait for God to bring about what He wanted for her; after all, He is so good. As a song that Jim enjoyed listening to said, "The miles of my journey have proved my Lord true." She will, indeed, never doubt that again.

"Lord, before I leave, may I ask you a question?"

"Go ahead, Nan. What is it you want?"

---

[41] I had Jesus make a play on words with Nancy, because one of the songs sung at here funeral was "Finally Home" written by Don Wyrtzen. Finally Home - Wyrtzen - YouTube

"When I leave you, I don't have to say goodbye each time, do I? Since I got here, I have always felt your presence, making me aware that you are never far from me. I never really leave you, do I?"

"You are learning quickly, Nancy. I'm eager for you to learn the depths of my being, how I relate and communicate with you. As that happens, you will understand what I want you to become. After all, I am your example of how we want to develop your life. You will always find our relationship to be very satisfying. I have a lot in store for you, Nancy. You will not be disappointed. By the way, I spoke with Asriel a little while back, and he told me to give you his greetings. He said he had fun bringing you home. He's been looking in on Jim and said he would be ready to come home soon. I know you are eager to see him."

As Nancy walked out, she thought, "I just met with God, and He spoke to me as a friend. I felt no fear. There was no feeling of inferiority or that I was in any way unimportant. How can I be so close to the Maker of the Universe and not feel inferior? I don't think I will ever be able to comprehend how great His love is for us. One thing I do know is that I sure enjoy being loved by God." With that, she smiled and walked on, contemplating her time with Jesus.

Fellowship

Spiritual power comes out of inward fellowship with God and abandonment to his purposes.
E. Stanley Jones
* * * * * * * * *

Just the privilege of fellowship with God is infinitely more than anything that God could give. When he gives himself, he gives more than anything else in the universe.
Frank Laubach
* * * * * * * * *

Aloneness can lead to loneliness. God's preventative for loneliness is intimacy - meaningful, open, sharing relationships with one another. In Christ, we have the capacity for a fulfilling sense of belonging, which comes from intimate fellowship with God and with other believers.
Neil T Anderson

Heaven is a real place. The more we know about it, the more we should anticipate it. As I have often suggested, Heaven is a prepared place for prepared people.
Don Piper

How you think about Heaven affects everything in life - how you prioritize love, how willing you are to sacrifice for the long term, how you view suffering, what you fear or don't fear.
John Burke, Imagine Heaven

Chapter Five -- Nancy's Life Portrayed

IT SEEMED LIKE ONLY A FEW EARTH DAYS, but it could have been a hundred earth years. Nancy couldn't tell because time and life are so different in heaven. It didn't matter because her existence is never-ending, not limited by time to curtail the enjoyment of life and the discovery of the greatness of God.

[*As I talk about heaven, I don't know how to represent time there. Will God designate time by days and hours as here on earth? There will be no nights[42] to separate the days in heaven. There will be no sunsets, sunrises and no need for a clock to keep time. We won't need sleep, so how do we distinguish what we know as time now? However, when speaking of the fruit on the tree of life, it says there is a new fruit each month.[43] So, for the sake of the book, let's keep with the familiar and talk about the progression of time like days.*]

Nancy mused one day about all the things that had happened since she arrived. The meet and greet was such a heartwarming and encouraging time. It was not long after that when she had a tour of her specially designed residence. She smiled as they asked her if she wanted anything changed in the decoration of her new home. After looking around, she commented that she wished to have nothing changed. It seemed like the person who decorated it thoroughly knew her tastes. She mused that such detail had to be from Jesus' intimate knowledge of me.

Her mind then went to her new mode of travel, and the first time she went somewhere at the speed of thought. It was disorientating at first, but she is now used to it. Every day was bringing new adventures and learning experiences into her life. She liked that.

---

42 Revelation 21:25; 22:5 "And there shall be no night there…" KJV

43 "On each side of the river stood the tree of life, bearing twelve crops of fruit, yielding its fruit every month." Revelation 22:2

One day Nancy received a message notifying her that the delegation that Jesus mentioned was coming to see her. She was delighted because she always enjoyed getting to know her fellow citizens. There were millions of people, and she just wanted to take her time getting to know them all.

Nancy liked to entertain, and so she decided she would prepare some fruit and freshly baked rolls, along with sweetbreads for her guest. She didn't know the delegation's plans but knew it would take some time. She also had a variety of drinks to offer her guests. Soon after everything was fashionably set out, the delegation arrived. There were about 60 in all. She appreciated the house's design to entertain larger gatherings.

After making the introductions, Nancy was amazed to learn that George Handel headed this delegation. George introduced everyone and their expertise and then told her the intent of their gathering.

"Nancy, I'm sure you remember when Jesus told you that He wanted to honor you. I know that you are familiar that this honor is a unique recognition of how your life brought glory to God and how He worked in and through you during your life. Jesus asked us to come up with unique ways to showcase your life and the glory it brought Him."[44]

"How would you like me to help you with this project, George? I know back on earth I would have been embarrassed to be honored,

---

44 This concept of God honoring His children so their story can honor Him is based on Matthew 26:6-13. This is the account of the woman anointing the feet of Jesus with expensive perfume; Jesus said that she shall be honored wherever the gospel is preached. *"Truly I tell you, wherever this gospel is preached throughout the world, what she has done will also be told, in memory of her."* The other basis for this honoring is an extension of the crowns God awards to His faithful followers. God loves His people, their lives have honored Him, and it very well could be that God will use our stories, in some way, to declare His glory, greatness, and love. Think of all the unique stories that will be the source of praise to God in various ways. Also consider: Matthew 25:21 "His master said to him, 'Well done, good and faithful servant. You have been faithful over a little; I will set you over much. Enter into the joy of your master.' (NIV)

but I know that this honor is to glorify the Lord Jesus, and I am looking forward to cooperating in every way possible."

George was eager as he continued to share further details, "Our purpose today is to listen to your life story. Tell us how your family and other people influenced you for the Lord. Share your salvation experience and your various ministry experiences over the years with Jim and your daughters at each church. Tell us about your struggles, trials, difficulties, and the lessons God taught you. We are interested in the great things and those instances that seem insignificant, for they are all part of your story. It helps us get a fuller picture of your life that leads to the glory of God. Tell us as much as you can about those who influenced your life. You were a faithful student of the Word. God delights when you declare how His Word influenced you in navigating those issues that came into your life."

George went on with his explanation, "To enhance the understanding of what happened in your life, our Lord will show you how people in your past, both those you knew and even those you never met, had an indirect influence on you. We waited this long because everything hasn't played out in how you influenced others through your life. Some of your noteworthy accomplishments came because of the influence of previous generations. Your powerful impact on your children is still playing out with your grandchildren and great-grandchildren in ways you never dreamed possible."

Nancy was excited to tell the story of her walk with God, even though she did not recognize how involved God was in her life as these events took place. As interviewers helped her identify God's work during her life, everything became clear in her mind. In heaven, her perception of God's involvement in her life on earth became so apparent. She was able to look back and recognize His participation in and through her walk of faith. The eyes of her understanding opened quickly to God's working as she started to rehearse her life. As a result, her excitement grew as she told her story.

There is no getting weary physically or emotionally in heaven, so discussions can continue until they are complete. Getting weary was a thing of the past. Her interview and others sharing their stories went on for what she imagined to be about three earth weeks. Everyone asked her questions about her life. These people had a knack for pulling out details she overlooked or thought insignificant at first. From personal experience, they knew the kinds of things that would honor God. That didn't mean that they didn't follow several rabbit trails to share thoughts of their own life so Nancy could identify with them. Newcomers did not always recognize the apparent working of God at first.

During the interview, she discovered the various talents of the delegation. The delegation consisted of 10 artists, four sculptors, nine playwrights, three set designers, two costume designers, eight authors, 20 music composers and songwriters, three music conductors, and a director who would oversee any talent production and make sure everything was accurate and coordinated. Realizing the diversity of the talents of her interviewers, she had to ask her questions.

"Why did she need so many kinds of talented people interviewing her?"

George was delighted to explain why this wide variety of talented people assembled to conduct her interview.

"Nancy, to express the creativity God gave each of us gifts, abilities, talents, and passions on earth. When we died and came here, we did not lose those interests and skills. These abilities blossomed and became more intense because we are no longer subject to sin and earthly limitations. Part of the benefit of possessing God's image is that our creativity is constantly looking for expression, and when we are inspired, we can't stop working. All of us are going to use our creative ability to honor you by accurately depicting the way you served God and honored our Savior. That is why we want to hear the details of your story. The ultimate purpose of our existence is to give tribute to God, our Savior, as we depict in some way what you did. The beauty of all of this is that our work, with our unique talents, will distinctively honor Jesus.

"Getting to know you not only helps us develop a relationship with you but allows us to come up with inspiring ideas of how to express your life in artistic ways. The painters and sculptors will depict specific incidents in your life by your work and influence on people. The painters will tell a story through their art that will capture the hearts of those who view them. I would say that we should have no fewer than 2-300 pictures and sculptures. Some of the sculptures will be set outside along streams and ponds. Our writers will present stories of your life and your influence on others. This work is part of the idea Jesus has for honoring those who have earned crowns for their faithfulness.

"We have several playwrights to produce plays and productions about specific incidents in your life that honor God in a particular manner. Once they write the scripts about portions of your life, we will choose a director to put together their support staff. They will enlist actors, musicians, stage people, and everyone needed to produce several open-air theater productions that will present your story to residents in the vast reaches of the universe.

"The songwriters will compose songs and write music that talks about those emotional times in your life when you came to understand God in more profound ways. We will include such things as the birth of your children and your influence on their lives. Then, we'll talk about your marriage to Jim and your ministry with the women at the churches you influenced through your fellowship and teaching. Let's not forget your involvement in the directing of children's ministries. Of course, we must mention your love for music and how you influenced others. Some leaned over your shoulder in the choir to listen to you sing because you were so good at reading music. You encouraged them with your ability and attitude. Your involvement in each of these people helped them grow in their faith and affected lives for the Lord.

"God loves to honor His children, but we realize that all of our lives have a greater purpose of honoring God. That is the ultimate end of each of these productions. People will sing our songs throughout eternity and by you at various celebrations and by the people you influenced for the Lord. That will make the way they honor God very personal."

George smiled and had a glimmer in his eye as he continued, "Every one of us has the opportunity to serve the Lord as we work on our part of one or several of the productions or presentations. Your life story, and those we interview, will also influence the presentations we produce. Here in heaven, we discovered that we all work together so well. No longer are we plagued with competitive egos or sinful pride that prevents us from listening to others and working together. We share ideas and can talk freely about them and work out the best solution. None of us feels we have to promote ourselves or show we are better than others. The result is that we have a wonderful, dynamic, working relationship in which we love serving the Lord together. We don't always agree on the details of certain productions but can work it out, even though it may take a while. Our creativity gives us such pleasure, and we find that working together helps bring out the best in us and helps us learn more about each other."

"You see, Nancy, even in heaven, we follow rabbit trails in our conversations. I do enjoy talking with God's people. Now let me finish sharing our ideas about your production. Your story will be longer than some because of your devotion to the Lord., Your lifelong service to Him gives us material upon which to draw.

George was pensive for a moment and then continued. "Some people came to know the Lord but never did much for Him, so they will not have much written about them. They didn't take their spiritual gifts, talents, abilities, and passions seriously to use them to serve God. Their stories will focus on God's grace. He sought to woo them into a closer walk, but they chose to live selfishly. As a result, their ability to honor God with their life is minimal. Even though they come empty-handed, their salvation is not inferior.

They entered heaven fully and warmly received as full members of God's family. Salvation is a gift received by grace through faith. Salvation came the same way for every believer, but salvation results differ significantly. Their self-centeredness caused them to seek earthly rewards rather than heavenly honors. Even though this saddens God, it doesn't prevent Him from being faithful in accepting them. But God's acceptance won't reward them for their lack of faithfulness. Paul tells us that these believers will suffer loss. "If anyone's work is burned up, he will suffer loss, though he himself will be saved, but only as one escaping through the flames."[45] However, we know our Lord loves them wholeheartedly and without reservation, for they are precious to Him because He died for them. God's forgiveness and resulting reconciliation that they accepted means they won't have to feel their unfaithfulness will minimize their importance in God's family.

"By the way, Nancy, we know that you enjoy singing. We would like to have you perform some songs about your experiences. Then when we display the paintings, we would like you to tell some of the stories of the impact of your ministry on people. We will also ask these people to share their side of the story."

There will be some musical productions of Nancy's life during the next few years. However, it will not stop there. God will bring ideas to mind to the writers and producers for new songs and theater productions to develop different aspects of her life and improve their experiences and abilities. In heaven, we will continue to mature.[46] As a result, we will look at things differently. Creative people will be inspired with new ideas to honor the Lord in the eons to come. Just as we increase in the capability of expressing our abilities on earth as we

---

45 "For no one can lay any foundation other than the one already laid, which is Jesus Christ. If anyone builds on this foundation using gold, silver, costly stones, wood, hay or straw, their work will be shown for what it is, because the Day will bring it to light. It will be revealed with fire, and the fire will test the quality of each person's work. If what has been built survives, the builder will receive a reward. If it is burned up, the builder will suffer loss but yet will be saved—even though only as one escaping through the flames." 1 Corinthians 3:11-15
46 Remember, the God that we are becoming like is infinite, so He is capable of the continual development and improvement of our being through all eternity. This thought deserves more than a footnote, for it assures a constant freshness to life. 2 Corinthians 3:18

mature, our creativity continues to grow to new heights in heaven. None of the residents will ever grow weary of learning about God's ingenious ways that He worked in the lives of His people. When you consider that millions upon millions of people are here, you can see that our task will take a long time. The thought of eternity is undoubtedly fantastic and exciting.

Praise from Hell?

Here is another thought. It is obvious how God works through His children's lives to develop and mature them through their life. Are there not millions of good reasons to honor and praise God through the lives of those who rejected Him? He provided redemption for all humanity and sought them out, but they rejected Him. All will sing about how God was gracious and kind to those who rejected Him, despite His effort to win them over.

The only reason I even allude to this is what Paul wrote in Philippians 2. The fallen angels and humans in hell will never cease to suffer torment, and yet in their suffering, they will have no choice but to acknowledge God's faithfulness, provision, and glory. They will declare that God is holy and just in their condemnation and separation from Him and the saints for eternity. In hell, *"every knee will bow, and every tongue will confess that Jesus is Lord to the glory of the Father."*[47] Why would that only happen one time? Might that echo from the citizens of hell at different times through eternity? Even though the citizens of hell rejected God, they will not be able to withhold their tongue from praising Him for the good He did for them. He showed them His love that was revealed through the death of Christ and then offered them complete salvation. Even though they rejected all of God's provisions, He blessed them with good things in life. I'm not saying this will happen, but if the rocks can cry out, it stands to reason that the unreconciled could also. The only objection that comes to mind

---

47 Philippians 2:9-11 "Therefore God exalted him to the highest place and gave him the name that is above every name, that at the name of Jesus every knee should bow, in heaven and on earth and under the earth, and every tongue acknowledge that Jesus Christ is Lord, to the glory of God the Father."

about the validity of this view is what Jesus said when He cast out demons during His earthly ministry. He wanted no recognition from them as to who He was. (Mark 1:34) He did not want their testimony to be the verification of His deity.

A Heavenly Glimpse

Will things happen this way in heaven and hell? I don't know. However, the concept presented in this chapter is crucial, and biblically holds many possibilities. People know we will honor the Father, Son, and Holy Spirit in heaven. It is hard for some to wrap their minds around the idea that we will find enough different reasons and ways in which to praise God. Is there going to be enough variety to hold our interest? You all know what it is like to appreciate the same song after listening too many times. What was once really interesting and exciting loses its hold on your interest after hearing it repeatedly.

Think of every person who has lived. Then recognize how God has worked in their lives in unique ways, not just once but thousands of times. It will not be hard to find ways to honor God through many of those situations. You can well understand then how there are sufficient resources to find an endless supply of topics to provide expressions to worship, adoration, praise, and thanks to God in music, literature, and art. That is what I sought to accomplish in telling the story about Nancy. She is but one in the millions who will be in heaven.

Some might think even with presenting praise in these various ways, won't musicians run out of melodies and words to use in their expressions of adoration? Think about the many thousands of songs, hymns, and spiritual songs written, along with musical scores used by believers in worship services and concerts. Every year we hear new Christmas music, songs that testify how He works in lives or has given life meaning. We will continue to find new and fresh ways to worship and praise God on earth. Themes for our songs don't run out because our songs come from a living relationship with God. Since that is true on earth, heaven will demonstrate even more creativity because of greater intimacy with God. The wellspring of God's qualities to adore will never run dry, for just as His mercies are new every day on earth,

His love knows no bounds. His resourcefulness will be full of surprises that genuinely delight us. There will be a constant resource of opportunities to express worship or praise to our God.

Our earthly comprehension of God grew before we got to heaven. In heaven, our understanding of God will be explosive and allow us to grow and expand our knowledge of God in a more realistic grasp of His glory. Our comprehension of God will continue to grow. It will reflect itself in the themes of our worship, praise, and understanding of God.

In this chapter, I talked about various ways praise and adoration of God will be developed and expressed in heaven. I sought to open your imagination to what it could be like there. The performances taking place in heaven will all be fantastic. God has wonderfully gifted people to compose songs of praise. Over the years, I heard of many concerts coming to our area. I often thought I would like to go to them, but more often than not failed to attend. However, when I did attend, I came away enriched and blessed. I can't imagine heaven being less dynamic or beautiful in the worship of Creator God.

Are you interested in going to a concert to hear the best of all singers and instrumentalists? It's coming your way. Don't miss it. It will be unlike anything you ever heard. Make your reservations now for this heavenly concert! If you delay your decision too long, you may miss out altogether. Tickets are a gift of God included when you take God up on His salvation offer.

The Believer's Rewards

God offers rewards to all believers. The believer earns these rewards when they learn to work with God and develop their gifts, abilities, and talents as they serve Him. He may call you to serve him at work, in your neighborhood, in your church, and always in your family. God has equipped you for service, don't neglect your opportunity to make an impact for eternity. If you have any inclination that the way you live life does not affect your rewards, then take the time to read 1 Corinthians 3:11-16.

* * * * * * * * *

2 Timothy 4:8 "From now on, there is stored up for me the **CROWN OF RIGHTEOUSNESS**, which the Lord, the righteous judge, will give to me on that day; and not to me only, but also to all those who have loved His appearing."

* * * * * * * * *

1 Corinthians 9:25-27 (WEB) "Every man who strives in the games exercises self-control in all things. Now they do it to receive a corruptible crown, but we an **INCORRUPTIBLE**. I, therefore, run like that, as not uncertainly. I fight like that, as not beating the air, but I beat my body and bring it into submission, lest by any means after I have preached to others, I myself should be rejected."

* * * * * * * * *

1 James 1:12 (ESV) "Blessed is the man who remains steadfast under trial for when he has stood the test he will receive the **CROWN OF LIFE**, which God has promised to those who love him."

* * * * * * * * *

1 Peter 5:2-4 "Care for the flock God has entrusted to you. Watch over it willingly, not grudgingly—not for what you will get out of it, but because you are eager to serve God. Don't lord it over the people assigned to your care, but lead them by your own good example. And when the Chief Shepherd appears, you will receive the **CROWN OF GLORY** that does not fade away."

* * * * * * * * * *

1 Thessalonians 2:19 (WEB) "For what is our hope, or joy, or **CROWN OF REJOICING**? Is not it even you, before our Lord Jesus at his coming?"

Look, I am coming soon! My reward is with me, and I will give to each person according to what they have done. Revelation22:12 NIV

Chapter Six -- Pursuing Our Passions

GOD MADE US COMPLEX BEINGS. Because God made us in His image, He equipped us well to continue to have an ever-expanding life potential. We noticed in the previous chapter that one of the ways we display the image of God is through our creativity. We see God's inventiveness in the wide variety of artistic abilities He implanted in us. God's creativity has infiltrated every area of our being. People are creative in a million different ways. Notice how a gardener will develop their flower gardens with just the right plants and greenery beautifully arranged. Another, having the same ability, will build something very different but beautiful to behold. Observe how the landscaper surrounds buildings with just the right flowers, trees, shrubs, stones, and ponds or streams. Another landscaper will decorate the same building in a totally different manner. The architect sees in his mind the unique qualities of a particular building and knows the kind of details needed to enhance its beauty.

One of the programs I've enjoyed watching over the years is Modern Marvels on the History Channel. That program makes me dream as they show the construction of large buildings, bridges, dams, and even the development of islands. These projects all needed competent people with talents in structural design, building skills, and problem-solving abilities to build them and recognize the environmental challenges they would face. Without exception, each project was also a work of art when completed.

The design is only the first stage of building any structure. Management brings in skillful workers to make the project a reality. Special equipment may need to be designed and manufactured or specially trained workers to do the job effectively. Job skills vary more than most of us can imagine for designing and building one of these large, creative structures. Let me point to some designers and projects to admire their artistry and awe-inspiring beauty.

Take, for instance, Frank Lloyd Wright[48] and his ability to make his buildings harmonize with their surroundings. He built one of his houses over a waterfall with trees growing through parts of the structure to add to its beauty.

The designers of the Palm Tree Island in Dubai[49] built an island in the shape of a palm tree capable of housing 120,000 residents. They used 32 million cubic meters of ocean sand to develop the island. They worked through many difficulties to bring this island into existence, and it became a beautiful community in which to live.

Stories of the tallest building in the world always present challenges. Notice the beauty of these skyscrapers on the web page.[50] Perhaps you have seen one of these skyscrapers built on Modern Marvels. Marvels show the problems they faced in erecting these buildings. These structures had an absolute beauty and splendor and exhibited magnificent artistry when completed. Often these buildings become landmarks, bringing pride to the community.

It takes people of varied skills to develop bridges that cross gorges and large bodies of water. Along with that comes the challenge of severe weather, powerful currents, and high winds. Yet as the engineers worked together and studied the problems, they could design and build incredible bridges that serve people well. Many of them display a new beauty that adds to the landscape.[51]

The largest dams[52] in the world required massive engineering feats. The work begins with diverting water, getting concrete to dry, providing new waterways for shipping traffic. They protect the environment by developing waterways for fish to continue traveling up

---

48 Enjoy the many pictures of his creations.
https://www.google.com/search?q=frank+lloyd+wright+homes&safe=active&source=lnms
&tbm=isch&sa=X&ved=0ahUKEwi1rMqK7LDSAhWE44MKHdRLADcQ_AUICCgB&bi
w=1366&bih=638
49 http://www.cntraveler.com/stories/2015-11-23/the-real-story-behind-dubai-palm-islands
50 http://www.worldatlas.com/articles/10-tallest-buildings-in-the-world.html
51 http://www.digitaltrends.com/cool-tech/biggest-bridges-in-the-world/#/4-4
52 http://top101news.com/2015-2016-2017-2018/news/world/biggest-dams-world/

and down the river. The designers loved the challenge, for it taxed their reasoning ability to the limit, yet they never gave up and gained tremendous satisfaction from completing the project. It was a joy for them to provide a functional dam to supply electrical power for the surrounding population and other benefits to their society.

Every one of the building projects required its people to exercise creativity, imagination, intelligence, problem-solving skills, and tenacity to complete the project. Such talent is not limited to the last couple hundred years, but man has displayed such creative abilities and the skills to carry them out throughout history. What makes us think that God will take these abilities and desires away from those who enter heaven with these God-given skills? Also, why would God remove the challenges that designers and builders of dreams must address?

Heaven is a place for people with such skills to continue to express themselves. When God created the earth, it was with the purpose of humanity using the skills that He implanted in them. Why would we think that God would take away these skills in heaven? It seems logical that He will continue to provide the opportunity to display these skills, talents, abilities, and desires in heaven. Projects may be vastly different from on earth but need skillful works. As they do these works, they understand the capability of God in doing the work and the joy that comes from completing such projects.

When Jesus tells us about heaven, He talks of constructing this massive condominium in heaven. *"In my Father's house are many rooms; if it were not so, I would have told you. I am going there to prepare a place for you."*[53] Jesus may do the work or be the architect overseeing the project using His skilled workers to build this place.

This unique place is the New Jerusalem, and its dimensions are in Revelation 21:26. *"The city lies foursquare, its length the same as its width, and he measured the city with his rod, fifteen hundred miles; its length and width and height are equal."*[54] Did you get the

---

53 John. 14:3

54 The Holy Bible: New Revised Standard Version. (1989). (Revelation 21:16). Nashville:

measurements of that city? It is a 1500-mile cube. Let me put that into perspective that you can better understand. Suppose 20 billion people went to heaven. That is more than having lived so far. There would be enough area for each person to have a "dwelling place" that is 75 acres large in this city. That still leaves room for parks, gardens, gathering places, and even shopping malls! To help you digest this, an 80-acre farm is one-half mile long by a quarter-mile wide.

"Honey, we have company coming next week!"
"How many dear?"
"About 150."
"No problem, we have plenty of guest rooms in our condo."
* * * * * * * * * * * *

The New Jerusalem will be the home base for God's family where they can hang out with God's children. It will be their meeting place to gather and talk after their explorations as they share their experiences and new findings of God. Every distant galaxy will reveal different aspects of God's glory. Instead of bringing goods or souvenirs back, they return with a deeper understanding of new facets of God from which flows new praise and adoration. They meet back here to share. The Bible says God will make a new earth for humanity to inhabit.[55] We base this claim on the promises God gave Israel that they would be in their land forever.[56]

Allow me to continue the development of the thought I was pursuing. If God gave people these creative abilities, and there is building going on in heaven, it would not be out of place to think that God will continue to allow development within His realms. He put this ability and desire in people to design and develop, so why should He not turn them loose in heaven or the universe? There will be a lot of opportunities to use their talents to build magnificent structures in

Thomas Nelson Publishers.
55 Then I saw "a new heaven and a new earth," m for the first heaven and the first earth had passed away, and there was no longer any sea.
56 Genesis 13:15, Exodus 32:13, Joshua 14:9, Jeremiah 17:4, Ezekiel 37:25

God's Kingdom. Each planet may offer different minerals and building materials to develop and use.

Think about being involved in some of these large construction projects with no financial or building material limitations. Consider working with a crew who seeks to bring out the best in each other and never tries to build their ego to finish the project on time. Instead, all have the same goal of developing a magnificent structure for the glory and honor of God.

There is more to consider. You need workers to bring the project into reality. These men are skilled. I lived in Flint, Michigan, area for almost three decades. General Motors (GM) pulled out of the city, closed most manufacturing facilities, and demolished the vacant buildings. When GM closed those plants, they also left a highly skilled workforce, many of who no longer had a place to work.

Something else plagued GM, as in other manufacturing plants, GM had its share of lazy workers, some of whom were addicted to drugs or alcohol, and the result was that they did not do their work. Some even skipped out of work because their building was so large they could hide from their bosses. They would clock in and spend the day in a local restaurant with friends. Most of the workers were not this disloyal to the company. GM had to deal with lazy employees who did not give them an honest day's work. I heard many dishonorable employee work stories while living in that area.

In heaven, there will not be any incompetents doing the work. People will be dedicated to the cause because they will be devoted to their Savior and Lord and will always choose to work and do their best to honor Him. They will be skilled, creative, and honest. Everyone will get along with each other as they work on the tasks. Remember, all God's people will display the fruit of the Spirit, and the foremost one is love. They will serve one another, respect each other, and get along without having unresolved differences.

Just as there is great pride in doing a good job, everyone will be joyful and delighted as they finish each building project for the Lord.

How would you like to be a team member working on one of those great projects for the Lord? No one will be insignificant on these building projects, for each person will work to their ability and receive proper honor. All will take pleasure in what they do. The goal of each worker will always be to do their best to glorify God through their abilities.

Will God have building projects for those who have this interest? God, in his creativity, designed and built or brought into being the earth, stars and planets, and all the animal kingdom. Do you think He will allow His servants to build structures to serve His children as they travel? God equipped many of His children with skills because it is part of His image. Why would He not allow them to use it?

Those in hell who have this gifting will want to use their creativity in some meaningful way, but they will lack the opportunity. They will have the desire and want to express the passion in their hearts but will not participate in anything that will give them such pleasure again.

It makes sense that if God gave this ability to people who are His children, He would provide challenging and magnificent projects to exercise their skills as a way of glorifying Him. What an exciting thought that makes our eternity more exciting and innovative. God has a vast eternity in store for us. It will be beyond our wildest imagination. The teaching of this chapter is essential, for if it is true, it also applies to all the other giftings God has distributed among the human race.

As I write this portion of the book, it is the week after the Star Wars Movie "Rogue One" came out. I saw it twice over the past week. This movie is about the development of the Death Star, which is a war machine as big as a planet or moon. They developed it with the capability to destroy a planet. The ship has this destructive capacity to bring the rebellion into submission. When you stand back and look at what they built, you recognize it as an amazing ship with colossal destructive capabilities. Star Wars is only a science fiction movie, and there is no reality in what they present.

In contrast, can you imagine our God, who has no limits, providing us with opportunities to get to know Him and His exceptional abilities by giving us fantastic and awesome projects on a scale as mentioned above to build? Participating in such a project is an example of discovering an aspect of His greatness. I can see God with a smile on His face as He sets before engineers and workers, such as building projects. The finished results will astound us as the project progresses. Completing this task brings awe to the workers and those who see it. People will see the finished project as a work that glorifies God.

This chapter focused on the idea of building. Many men and women take great pleasure in designing, building, decorating, and bringing a project to completion. God may very well use our fascination for the building trades to continue to challenge our imagination and give us great joy in building unique and challenging projects. After all, He put that ability and interest in us, and we will know that our skills continue to be of value to God. Contemplating such ideas help us recognize that heaven will have work that will capture our imagination, creativity, and joy in serving.

Should building projects take place without any complications? Will work happen in heaven without people having to work through problems and complications? Why do we think God won't allow snags in work projects to provide opportunities for people to grow in their abilities and problem-solving skills? We solve difficulties by facing challenges and working with a team of talented people with various skills. Solving problems draws people together and creates great satisfaction when they finish the job. The result is that these people become closer friends as they problem-solve together. Besides, there are stories to tell to friends afterward.

I trust that I have given you some possible ways to consider the joy of being in heaven. The more we can discuss real-life issues of our actions, the more it will captivate our attention and interests. Let your imagination run wild about how our resourceful God wants us to come to know Him in ways that fulfill the desires of our souls. God will undoubtedly allow us to express these passions when we get to heaven.

After all, God implants within us the kinds of interests, talents, and abilities that captivate our attention now.

What would you like to participate in to get your creative juices flowing when you get to heaven? You might say music and art are sweet, but not interesting to me. Designing and building magnificent structures all over the universe isn't the kind of work that captivates my attention.

If I had my druthers, you might say…

Chapter Seven -- I'd Rather Go Fishing

GREG WAS A STONEMASON. Craig was a chemist for GM and loved his work. However, if you allowed these men to do what they wanted, they would choose fishing. Oh, to enjoy a beautiful day on the lake catching fish when no one is around to bother you. It's time to think and enjoy God's creation.

If you listen to a person who likes to fish, you may hear him say something like this: "Let me be alone on the lake near a good fishing hole. I enjoy sport-fishing and look for fish with a little bit of fight in them. I'm a good host because I always delight in taking the fish home for a tasty dinner afterward."

Many anglers enjoy being out on the lake or the challenge on the sea as they seek a good catch. When waiting for the fish to bite, they can have some quiet, productive time. The angler observes the water, notices the movement of the fish, and discerns his surroundings. Nothing compares to the beautiful trees surrounding the lake and watching the local wildlife come for a drink or be playful with each other. This time is precious to the angler, for it is a time to reflect and talk with God. No longer will God be quiet in our conversations with Him, for He will actively participate and answer our questions or chat with us. Jesus found it essential to get away in the hills to be alone with His Father. God's anglers value this time alone with God as they enjoy His creation. Like the travelers on the Emmaus road, they will think about their time with the Lord as they were fishing and say in their heart, "Were not our hearts burning within us while he talked with us…[57]"

---

[57] Luke 24:32

Eating in heaven

The above scenario brings up another question. Will we eat in heaven? Jesus ate with the disciples after the resurrection.[58] Eating is significant because Jesus was in His resurrection body when he did so. Also, we find that when Jesus gathers His bride to Himself, He will welcome the saints with a great wedding feast.[59] What do you see at a wedding feast? There is usually fantastic food and plenty of it. That was true in the culture in which Jesus lived and is part of our tradition as well. To strengthen this argument, we need to keep in mind that there will be fruit trees for the nations to eat. In Revelation 22:1-2,[60] these trees have a specific purpose, and people come to eat from them. The tree of life will bear a new fruit each month.

Also, the book of Revelation describes the city's gates in a specific way. Notice John's description of the New Jerusalem. "*The twelve gates were twelve pearls, each gate made of a single pearl...*"[61] Pearls have only one source. They come from oysters. One can only imagine how enormous such an oyster must be to provide a pearl big enough for one of twelve city gates in 6,000 miles of wall.

I'm going somewhere with all of this. I'm using these teachings to verify what I said earlier about the fisherman eating their fish. I would think that eating has a place in heaven. Some may think we will only be vegetarians because eating living creatures means they would have to die. Others believe we will be able to partake of fish and meat. How did the oyster give up its pearl in the paragraph above without dying? I don't know what God's menu plans are, but the bottom line is that the Bible talks about food and eating in heaven.

---

58 Luke 24:40-43; John 21:4-12

59 Revelation 19:9 "Then the angel said to me, "Write this: Blessed are those who are invited to the wedding supper of the Lamb!" And he added, "These are the true words of God

60 "Then the angel showed me the river of the water of life, as clear as crystal, flowing from the throne of God and of the Lamb down the middle of the great street of the city. On each side of the river stood the tree of life, bearing twelve crops of fruit, yielding its fruit every month. And the leaves of the tree are for the healing of the nations"

61 Revelation 21:21

Perhaps the meals reference something delightful that will bring people together for fellowship opportunities with new or different believers in heaven.

"Hey Peter, I'd like some chips with another helping of fish, and don't skimp on the chips this time."

With a smile on his face, Peter replies, "Jim, I think I'm going to have you sit by the chips next time. That way, I can eat without your constant interruption."

Chefs and gardeners

Will the heavenly banquets appear out of nowhere? Perhaps God will use those with culinary skills to create exceptionally tasting meals for us on these special occasions. I do not think any of us will have to be weight watchers there. We will be able to enjoy the senses God gave us, such as taste, texture, and smell. I remember as a child coming into our house on a cold wintery afternoon after being outside on the farm and immediately smelling the bread or the pan of hot cinnamon rolls mom just made. Oh, how such smells imprint our memories. Get them out of that oven as fast as you can. I am hungry and want something to eat. Bill wants butter and strawberry preserves for his bread, and Jan wants the icing dripping off the cinnamon rolls. Doug wants seconds before he has his first taste. John likes his cinnamon roll plain with lots of frosting. Oh my, they all sound so good! I think God will allow us to discover many ingredients that are even more aromatic to tantalize our senses.

I know of a man who thought with his head in pursuing his degree to become a lawyer. After he passed the bar, he realized this occupation was not as fulfilling as imagined. Despite the debt he incurred in becoming a lawyer, he went to culinary school and became a chef. His training landed him a position in a children's hospital, preparing menus for the young patients who had debilitating or terminal diseases. Now he serves delicious, nutritious meals to children recovering from serious illnesses. Those children and parents so appreciated his expertise, which grabbed his heart. God puts in our hearts this desire to express our creativity and serve people. God wants us to have joy in what we do to serve others.

Perhaps some think that God may give them something to do in heaven that may not be exciting or challenging in an area that interests them. However, when we realize that the way God created us is an expression of Him in us, then there is no reason to think that He won't use that as a means of understanding Him uniquely in heaven. That thought of doing what we like, and realizing that it is a way we serve and get to know God, should grab our heart and imagination.

If your heart were in the culinary arts, then perhaps you would enjoy spending some time working with other great chefs in preparing for banquets and gatherings for God's people on special occasions. You may want to cook for your friends at special events. I've watched a lot of cooking shows over the years and noticed, after a while, that a lot of meals are only a remake of something familiar. People are always looking for new spices and diverse savors to tantalize their taste buds. I wonder how expansive God's pantry is for the cooks of heaven. Various spices would require gardens to cultivate, harvest, and prepare them for the cooks. Perhaps there will be a crew of botanists developing new plants and spices. As the cooks become acquainted with the various spices and foods, He will use their creative skills to produce extravagant and tasty spices, vegetables, and fruits for the cooks and those who partake.

I can cook, but I am not a good cook, nor am I very creative. However, I do like to eat. I look forward to experiencing the creativity of God's cooks and bakers in heaven. I'll be glad to taste-test whatever they prepare because I know they will make their foods flavorful and appetizing. They will give us their best. How can I go wrong with that? How about you, will you be part of the cooking crew or sit with me at the table? Remember, it is not just about the food, but it will be about the conversation with each other, and much of that will focus on the greatness and goodness of our Savior and friend, Jesus Christ. However, before I eat, you may hear me say:

"Hey Jesus, thanks for this food. It sure looks delicious and smells tantalizing; I can hardly wait to dig in. By the way, would you pass me one of those rolls in front of you?"

"Sure, Jim, I'd be glad to." With a smile, he grabs the roll and tosses it to me. "Good catch Jim. Enjoy!"

My friend, it will be that real. I trust you see heaven more imaginatively as you expand your thinking about the kinds of things we could be doing there. We will have such a great time with God there. Heaven will not be a long, dull church service but an experience of lively interaction, learning, and serving, to bring worship and praise to our creator. It will be a time to understand and experience the fullness of whom God is and what He made us be. It will be a life of growing, learning, experiencing life as God designed for us, and some of that may be around a table set with delicious food.

The scientific mind satisfied

Let's consider some other areas of interest. We started this chapter with Greg and his love of fishing. Others like fish as well as various kinds of wildlife. They are not interested in catching and eating them, but they want to understand all about them and their uniqueness in how God made them. These are not just scientists but ordinary folk who have observed fish and animals for years and want to learn more about their habits and design so they can see the intricate creativity God used in forming them. The more they learn, the more their growing understanding of God draws them to want to know His mind. They will continually be amazed at His creativity, attention to detail, and the wide variety of usefulness. They already know He is so intelligent and wise, so they study His designs in creation to discover the features of the expression of His wisdom, which in turn reveals His glory. They will never reach the limits of ascertaining God's genius as they observe all the benefits and originality in each animal, fish, insect, and bird. With their increased mental abilities, they will grasp ideas and purposes placed in the animal with a clearer understanding.

Our speaker's name was Dale, and he related an encounter with a scientist named Ellen while flying. Ellen told him how she devoted her life to understanding one particular aspect of a bird. The more she studied this bird, the more fascinating details she discovered, and she realized she had a lot more to learn. Ellen traveled to observe this bird in another country and seated herself next to Dale. He asked Ellen if she knew why she had such a desire to devote her life to learning about this particular aspect of the bird. She thought for a moment, and it began to dawn on her. She never thought about the 'why' of what she was doing. Her sparked interests led to a sharp curiosity that became her passion. She asked, "Why is it that I want to know so much about this bird?"

Dale explained that God put in us a curiosity to know Him by understanding His creation. In observing and studying such details, we see God's genius of the design and structure of each living thing. Each offers a new variety of differences and purposes. He spent several minutes detailing God's unparalleled ability to design living creatures with endless uniqueness. That draws so many to study and observe different parts of God's creation. The ultimate goal is that they get to know God and His ability. The woman responded, "Why has not anyone ever told me about this before?" He replied, "I just did."

God put in us a curiosity to know Him by understanding His creation.

That curiosity God placed in humanity is there because He created us in His image. It helps us to get to know and understand Him. In the human heart, there is an insatiable desire to comprehend God by studying the details of His creation. Even though sin clouds our divine image, our yearning heightens to know God through creation when delivered from sin's hold on our life. He will unfetter our longings to explore His genius. Time will no longer hold us back from learning. Our thinking process will significantly increase so it will be clear and accurate, thus allowing us to go into a deeper understanding of God and recognize minute details He designed into each part of His creations.

God is the creator of this world, and He programmed every detail of it. He created the universe, which includes all that is on planet earth. However, an unredeemed man looks for ways to take God out of the creation equation. Many attribute God's creative ability to man's theory of evolution. They credit the theory of evolution, driven by blind chance and dumb luck, in how all the plants, animals, fish, birds, and even humans came into being. They ignore the reality of the living God who shows His wisdom and power through His glorious creation.[62] Because some scientists seek to explain science with no thought of God, they belittle His glory and miss what God desires humanity to learn. They lose their sense of awe because they have denied God and the truth that He is the creator. Lies blind their eyes to His part in the incredible detail and design, expressing His imagination, power, purpose, and glory in creation.

You are not in heaven yet. Do you value seeing God in creation? I took a three-month road trip in 2015 and traveled to the western part of the United States. The beauty of the mountains, forests, and the splendor that water brought into the scenery was a constant source of my admiration. At one point, as I was observing God's creation, I wondered if God was thinking something like this as the flood receded: *"Let me see what kind of beauty I can bring about for humanity to enjoy, and thus see my power, workmanship, and creativity."* So He carved out the Grand Canyon, He pushed up the mountains of Yosemite Park, and He plumed Yellowstone with regular displays of geysers. (Old Faithful erupts every 60-90 minutes and heats to steam temperatures between 3700 – 8400 gallons of water.) In a lonely part of Idaho, he carved a canyon with a river and placed twin falls that still delight people today. God touched thousands of areas before the flood's conclusion, preparing His world for us to enjoy.

Many Christians say that God had a hand in evolution. That is not the same as saying God is the creator and designer of all things. God declares in the Bible many times that He is the creator.[63] The many

---

[62] "For since the creation of the world God's invisible qualities—his eternal power and divine nature—have been clearly seen, being understood from what has been made, so that people are without excuse." Romans 1:20

miracles in the Bible state that He has the needed power to do as He claims. Why is it so important to acknowledge that God is the creator of all things?

God declares in Revelation 4 His right to take over the earth and return it to His authority. Listen to the 24 elders as they proclaim this truth around the thrown. *"You are worthy, our Lord and God, to receive glory and honor and power, **for you created all things, and by your will, they were created and have their being.**"*[64] *(Emphasis mine)*

Recognizing God as the creator helps us see that He has authority over all things, and we should give Him His due glory and honor. Learn to be a creation observer, for that truth will be one of the focal points for understanding God's greatness. That brings us to the purpose of this book. If God wants us to understand specific aspects of Him on earth by observing His creation, why should that change when we get to heaven?

"For since the creation of the world, God's invisible qualities—his eternal power and divine nature—have been clearly seen, being understood from what has been made, so that people are without excuse."[65] Notice the qualities God wants us to learn about Him as we observe creation. He displays His boundless power in bringing about the formation of the universe and the world in it. What kind of power does it take to call everything into being? Just try speaking something into existence. Think about the size of the universe with billions of galaxies and stars beyond number, and God made them all. What could better display His divine nature than bringing all the universe and this world into being and sustaining it? Only an all-powerful, all-knowing, and all-wise creator could do such a thing. See also Psalm 19:1-6.

---

[63] Genesis 1:1; John 1:3; Genesis 2:4; Genesis 5:1; Deuteronomy 4:32; Isaiah 42:5; Isaiah 45:18; Malachi 2:10; Mark 13:19; Colossians 1:16; Job 4:17; 20:4; 26:7, 13; 33:4; 36:3; Ecclesiastes 11:5; 12:1; Isaiah 37:16; 40:28; 41:20; 42:5; 43:1; Jeremiah 10:12; 14:22; 31:35; 32:17; 33:2; Ezekiel 29:2; Romans 1:19-20, 25. Creation is an important issue in the Bible.
64 Revelation 4:11
65 Romans 1:20

The magnificence of God as creator jolted the scientific world in the late 1990s when it became apparent that not just the world but the whole universe is fine-tuned. Matter, energy, forces, gravity are in such exacting proportions that our universe could not have gotten here by accident. In 1997, scientists recognized 17 features of the universe that made it finely tuned for life. Now scientists have discovered over 200 finely tuned features of the universe.[66]

If gravity or the forces in atoms were even one percent more or less, we could not have many of the elements we need. Carbon is one of them and is a critical component of life. If the universe had dispersed a little bit faster, then we could not have the creation of stars. If it dispersed a fraction of a bit slower, then it would have collected too much mass, making everything so dense the universe would collapse on itself. One report said a slower dispersion of the gases would cause them to gather in black holes with a density of two billion tons per teaspoon. Such reasoning comes from scientists and is causing many to rethink the possibility of an intelligent creator. Many are seeing God's glory in the universe. It makes sense that the more man looks at God's creation, the better they will be able to see His fingerprints all over it.

One of the places I stopped during my three-month road trip was Hearst Castle in California. Hearst was a man who not only had money, but he had a love of history and art, which allowed him to bring it all together in his castle. I walked through his castle and was in total awe of how he brought all the beautiful acquisitions together. He knew what he wanted, went after his dream, and found a way to display art and history elegantly. I was one of the hundreds who went through the castle that day. One of the purposes of this tour was to show off the glory of William Randolph Hearst, not just by the fabulous interior but also by the stories of famous people and heads of state who spent time with him.

---

[66] Some examples can be found at:
https://www.discovery.org/m/securepdfs/2018/12/List-of-Fine-Tuning-Parameters-Jay-Richards.pdf -- Also: https://wng.org/roundups/a-fine-tuned-universe-1617224984

When it comes to celebrating one's glory, Hearst is only a preschooler compared to God's glory that He demonstrated in the creation of heaven and earth and all He has designed in them. Even though we do not recognize all of His glory now, we will comprehend it as we learn about His creation in the ages to come. The result will be that we will not be able to keep our mouths shut. We will jump for joy, raise our hands, and glorify the creator God. That is why He wants us to learn the intricate details of His creation. The purpose of understanding the aspects of His creation will be to proclaim God's glory so we can declare His praise.

You may sign up now to be on a study team or involved in a research project when you get to heaven. There is room for all who want to enlist. The only requirement is that you are reconciled with God to be an official citizen of heaven, and thus you become qualified to join any research team.

Biblical Description of Heaven

"The twelve gates were twelve pearls. Each one of the gates was made of one pearl. The street of the city was pure gold, like transparent glass. I saw no temple in it, for the Lord God, the Almighty, and the Lamb, are its temple. The city has no need for the sun, neither of the moon, to shine, for the very glory of God illuminated it, and its lamp is the Lamb. The nations will walk in its light. The kings of the earth bring the glory and honor of the nations into it. Its gates will in no way be shut by day (for there will be no night there), and they shall bring the glory and the honor of the nations into it so that they may enter." **Revelation 21:21-26**

"He showed me a river of water of life, clear as crystal, proceeding out of the throne of God and of the Lamb, in the middle of its street. On this side of the river and on that was the tree of life, bearing twelve kinds of fruits, yielding its fruit every month. The leaves of the tree were for the healing of the nations. There will be no curse any more. The throne of God and of the Lamb will be in it, and his servants serve him. They will see his face, and his name will be on their foreheads. There will no longer be any night, and they need no lamp light; for the Lord, God will illuminate them. They will reign forever and ever." **Revelation 22:1-5**

Chapter Eight –Nancy Greets her Sister

NANCY RECEIVED WORD that her sister Norma would arrive in five minutes. It was three years since she saw her. *"I'm so glad to have another family member home,"* she thought as she made her way to the welcome center. As Nancy entered, all her family and friends were talking with Norma. There was the usual excitement, hugs, laughter, and catching up. These times were always pleasurable.

Meet and greet lasted a little over three hours. Then, one by one, people left until it was just Nancy and Norma talking. Nancy stayed because she wanted to share with Norma things she learned about life in heaven, what was happening to her and her life portrayal project. After sharing for a while, Nancy just had to say something to Norma about the exciting features of heaven.

Nancy had difficulty containing herself because she had so much to tell Norma. Excitedly she started to share.

"Norma, life changes here in heaven. I'm sure you are noticing some of that already. One of the first things I noticed when I got here was that I had no more fear. I can fully express the person God created me to be. I don't feel I have to try to be someone I'm not. There were times I did things just because I thought someone expected me to, and I didn't want to let them down. I wasn't serving them out of my heart but misguided responsibility. I don't know how often I didn't say something because fear controlled me. Jim and I would talk, and I couldn't admit I was wrong. I was ashamed of the way God made me in some areas, so I refrained from talking to people or serving God when the Spirit prompted me."

"You will notice more fully how fear affected life and the influence it had on you. It prevented us from drawing close to God, kept us from being real in our relationships, and stopped us from doing things to enjoy life and serve God. Fear made us think the worst of others and caused us to be critical in our conversation to and about people. There's no more fear here, Norma."

"Nancy, slow down. I can see you are excited about the change you experienced. We have all eternity to catch up. Tell me some of the changes that you noticed the most."

"Norma, you will discover that life in heaven is so much more complex than we ever imagined. The angels have a greater diversity of responsibility than we realized. Through the eons of time, God has given them more significant duties in ruling and caring out responsibilities than ever entered our minds. As great as the angels are, we, along with other faithful believers, will help rule over them. That responsibility will include giving them learning assignments, bringing people together to share stories of God's involvement in their lives and the angelic involvement in our lives, and organizing corporate worship sessions. God gives us both freedom and responsibility in heaven. The teachers showed us the ways of Satan and his fellow powers of darkness who rule with him. No wonder we saw so much evil on earth. They knew God's plan for the final redemption of humanity and the earth, but their hatred of God and their evil nature would not relent in their opposition to God and His people."

"One of the truths we didn't take seriously on earth was that God will not be finished with earth at the end of the Kingdom age. He created this world for us to enjoy, which is why He renews the heavens and earth.[67] As I thought about why God would renew the earth, it made sense that God first designed it perfectly for us to enjoy. Then sin interrupted God's plans for humanity after a short

---

[67] Revelation 21:1 *"And I saw a new heaven and a new earth, for the first heaven and first earth had passed away and there was no longer any sea."*

period, and the program changed. We sure know some of what that entailed. Now God will inhabit the new earth with His children."

"God will also repopulate the new earth with all the familiar animals and new varieties. We will delight in exploring the depths of God's creation as well as enjoy its beauty. God showed His great wisdom in the details, beauty, and purpose of His creation, and He continues to want us to appreciate it and experience His handiwork first-hand. There will still be mountains, rivers, lakes, and waterfalls beyond imagination. Flowers, trees, plants, shrubs, and various fruits and vegetables will all be there to provide beauty to behold. We saw the incredible beauty of earth under the curse. It will be even more magnificent when God lifts the curse."

"You will discover this very soon. The greatest aspect of heaven I thoroughly enjoy is intimate fellowship with God. He hears our every thought and responds immediately. He expresses His love toward us freely. Love permeates the atmosphere of heaven. He reveals aspects of His being that cause great excitement in learning about Him. He wants us to allow our curiosity to discover truths about Him, so He still doesn't tell us everything about Himself or His glories in the universe. He wants us to discover them in the eons to come. He delights in pointing us in the direction that allows us to discover Him on our own. God doesn't take over and do everything for us but expects us to use our gifts, intellect, and abilities to discover new aspects about Him. Do you remember how Jesus often answered a question with a question? Jesus wanted people to think and reach a conclusion. The Father does the same thing. Furthermore, I have never experienced any emptiness here. God is my constant friend and companion, who is always with me. I never feel distant from Him. I feel that I constantly have His complete attention. That is what everyone up here says too. I'm learning something new and exciting about Him every day. And, do you know what else is exciting, Norma?"

"I think you're going to tell me no matter what I say, Nancy." She said with a knowing smile. That good-natured sibling bantering continues in heaven.

"Life keeps getting better and better. Every day I'm learning something new and going deeper in my understanding of God. The more I learn of Him, the more I want to know about Him. Getting to know Him never gets old, for it's always exciting and never stagnant, for there is no limit to the depth of His understanding, greatness, and display of His abilities. That then leads to praise of His greatness and faithfulness."

"We always knew we would learn more about God, but I am finding out more about myself as I learn about God. I am experiencing the depth of my ability to learn and comprehend. I can express His character, like the fruit of the Spirit, in ways that were so foreign to me on earth. My interest in discovering how things work and the intricacies of his creation are not a passion, and I can now comprehend how they work and see the depth of God's creativity and design.

After a short discussion concerning the impressive things she discovered about God, Nancy continued. People are not two-faced. They like hearing what we have to say. No one merely tolerates you here, but they enjoy the interaction and sharing their thoughts. It takes only a short time talking with them to feel like your best friend. I think it is because we have a shared love for God. It's fun conversing with the saints and angels because they freely share their hearts. Depth of intimacy in everyday conversation is a typical way of life here. You never have to worry about people lying or telling you partial truths. Honesty and openness are so refreshing. All conversations are in love and a desire to help others learn, even though you may not always agree with the person."

"We sure could have used a lot more of that on earth. Can you imagine how the church would have been a lot different if Christians spoke the truth in love? I know as Don and I served, one of the big hurts was that people who needed help would not be honest and admit it."

"Norma, you won't experience any of that here. Let me tell you about something else I've been enjoying. Perhaps it's a small thing, but it caused me a lot of frustration on earth. No longer do I struggle to remember a person's name. I don't have to fake it because I forgot their name or what we talked about during our last conversation. People are so open that you eagerly anticipate your next meeting with them. The relationship we longed for with people is completely fulfilling. Establishing meaningful relationships took a long time on earth, and we made very few of them. The intimacy we experience with our closest friends is commonplace with each person we meet. One of the common themes of our conversations is sharing what we recently learned about God. One person focuses on one aspect of God, and another is enamored with something none of us has yet considered. We help each other grow in appreciating different aspects of God, and praising God is the end result of such a discussion. Fellowship is always genuine and fulfilling, and we find ourselves talking about something different each time we get together. This kind of growing friendship is what God intended us to experience continually."

There was a pause in the conversation. The silence was no longer awkward. People aren't afraid to stop and think about the new information they need to assimilate. In that silence, they both looked around to admire the beauty of heaven and listen to joyful conversations coming from the streets. The calmness and joy of people captured their attention for a while.

"Norma, have you noticed new freedom in your spirit?"

"Absolutely! I do feel a freedom I've never experienced before. There are no more nagging doubts. Oh my, I never realized how many lies were part of my life. All the reasons I didn't trust God were that I believed lies so easily. Believing lies kept me from relating to people honestly, as I should have. It caused me to put up barriers and facades that were not real. Wow, having my sin nature eradicated sure makes a difference in how we act and see life, as well as how we perceive God."

"Norma, it just keeps getting better. I'm learning more every day about the goodness of God. Let me tell you about something else that happens here that I would never have imagined in a million years. God has a unique way to honor us for our faithfulness on earth. Do you remember studying the reward crowns[68] God gives to His people for faithfulness? Those crowns involve the honor that God bestows on His faithful people. Let me share how involved some of this recognition and honor is. You will find that when God does something, He always does it, first-class."

"Nancy, I've never seen you this excited about anything before. I can tell by your reaction that this will be a place that we will enjoy above any expectation that we had on earth. It saddens me that we didn't give heaven the priority for the hope that God intended. As I looked around, I noticed that it surely is a place beyond description. I'm eager to explore all the glories of heaven. Sis, I interrupted you, continue with your thought; I'm listening."

"It's not just what is happening to me. It's the people involved in the project. These people have great talent. We have such wonderful conversations, and they are a delight to work with on my project."

"Nancy, what in the world do you mean by 'your project?'"

"It is a life portrayal project. It depicts, through various media, my life and the people I influenced. Parts of my life portrayal deals with people who influenced me and even those whose influence has come through the ages to set the stage for my life. God delights in honoring us for our faithfulness. He will feature each person, who faithfully served God in a specific way, in their life portrayal."

---

[68] The Bible talks about five crowns He offers to the believer for faithfulness. They are the imperishable crown, the crown of rejoicing, the crown of righteousness, the crown of glory, and the crown of life. https://www.gotquestions.org/heavenly-crowns.html

"The interview process, by various artists, was lengthy. One group wrote a musical about my life. It is now complete, and they are working on its production. Do you know who headed my project? You'll never guess, so I'll tell you. It's George Handel. The presentation about my life is not a standalone composition but an integral part of a great symphony that shows the glory of God through the ages as He worked in and through individuals. God's work does not end after a generation or even ten but has come through the ages with purpose and will continue into eternity.

Nancy was excited as she went on to tell Norma about this section of her life musical. She continued with little hesitation.

"God wants me to tell about His involvement in my life from my perspective. He wants each presentation to be full of personal details. These productions become the basis of glorifying Him. Sharing from my viewpoint gives the story a personal perspective that honors Him uniquely. There was so much to talk about when you take into consideration how Jesus saved me, how the Holy Spirit transformed me, as well as God's guiding hand through my life."

Norma could see how excited Nancy was about this. She couldn't contain herself as she gave Norma all the details of what was happening. "Nancy, you have totally new freedom here. Heaven sure has certainly transformed you! Tell me more about this musical. Am I correct in assuming that they will feature not just Jim but our family in some way in this production?"

"I like that because the Christian life is never just about one person. You know how much I don't like the limelight."

Nancy went on. "Not every believer will be featured in a life presentation. That's because they loved the world more than God and did not take their faith seriously. For those of us who lived our faith, it's exciting to observe how the composers and writers interweave the details of our life into such beautiful compositions. The purpose of everyone's story is to honor God, and that pleases me. These composers have been working hard, and they are so talented. They learned the kinds of music that thrilled my soul and were able to use those styles and new ones to compose the lyrics and music for the presentations."

Nancy paused thoughtfully and then went on. "You would think that compositions would come together easily here, but that is not the case. God wants them to work on detail, and sometimes they have to rewrite a song 50 or 60 times before it reaches the desired quality. They told me that some composers put their compositions on a shelf for years until they came up with the proper inspiration to complete that part of the musical. Because they desire to honor the Lord, they always work to get the lyrics and music just right. They make sure not to present anyone as someone better than they were. That kind of dedication pleases me."

"Norma, as I told you, George Fredrick Handel is the head music writer for my composition. He and the other composers let me sit in on some of the sessions where they worked out the details of how lives come together in God's great plan. They don't just focus on music. They also commissioned artists to depict Jim's and my story in a huge mural painting about God's work among humanity. Each of us is significant to Him, and He wants to honor us in this musical."

"Nancy, when will this musical be presented? I am eager to hear it."

"Norma, if you think George Handel's Messiah was majestic and stirring, then you are in for a treat. God wants us to use lively music and a wide variety of styles and instruments to present this musical. I guess I got ahead of myself. When will the presentation be performed? It will be sometime after the conclusion of the Kingdom Age when Satan is imprisoned forever, never to bother humanity again."

"I wonder how long it will take to present something this massive, Nancy. Have you heard anything about that?"

"Sis, up here, we don't have to worry about time. It will be an open-air production, and we won't have to worry about sunburns or inclement weather that will shut it down. And guess what. There are no mosquitos here. There won't be any time constraints to limit us as on earth. This massive concert will have thousands of singers, instrumentalists, and songs that will exalt our Savior. The little I've heard has been breathtaking. I don't know how long it will take for the performance. Perhaps there will only be various segments presented at a time. We'll find out when it happens."

"By the way, Nancy, have you heard when Jim is going to arrive?"

"We don't get to know that, Norma. I didn't know you were coming until five minutes before your arrival. Although, I did hear at the reception that mom knew a few hours before your arrival. She sure was anticipating you. God likes newcomers to feel comfortable, so familiar people, such as family or friends, welcome them. Coming to a new place where they already know people make arrival much more comfortable."

"Hey, I know where mom and dad live. You know they aren't husband and wife here. Let's go over and get them. We can go out for coffee at the Living Water Café. Dad likes the pies there. You know he still uses his old joke about pie. He only likes two kinds of pie, hot and cold. We still have a lot more to catch up on, so let's do it now. Are you game?"

They both turned and walked out the door, talking to each other a mile a minute. Their old habit of talking to each other simultaneously and having no problem keeping up with what the other is saying did not change in heaven.

The Desire of Jesus expressed for us

"Do not let your heart be troubled. Believe in God. Believe also in me. In my Father's house are many dwelling places. If it weren't so, I would have told you, for I go to prepare a place for you. And if I go and prepare a place

for you, I will come again and will receive you to myself; that where I am, you may be there also. And you know where I am going, and you know the way."
John 14:1-4

Death is the doorway by which God invites us to something far better than anything in this life: personal fellowship with Him in heaven.
Erwin W. Lutzer

My Teaching on Heaven was Challenged

A man once responded to a post I made about heaven. He said, "Nowhere in the bible does it say that heaven is our home." He referred to our eternal dwelling as the New Jerusalem and the renewed earth on which we will reside. He also said Only God would be in heaven."

When someone makes a statement like that, I take the time to consider what he or she said. As I let the thought simmer in my mind, invariably Holy Spirit brings verses to mind scripture that allows me to understand the truth.

Philippians 3:20 says we will be in heaven. "But our citizenship is in heaven. And we eagerly await a Savior from there, the Lord Jesus Christ." NIV

John 14:2-3 "My Father's house has many rooms; if that were not so, would I have told you that I am going there to prepare a place for you? [3] And if I go and prepare a place for you, I will come back and take you to be with me that you also may be where I am." NIV

When someone challenges your understanding of faith, it will have Biblical backing if it is correct. Dig into God's word, and do not rely on your feelings or what someone told you. God's word tells us what we need to know.

Chapter Nine -- Play Ball

MANY YEARS AGO, I saw a short video about golf in heaven. It made golf seem quite dull. Every shot was a hole in one, no matter how the golfer connected with the ball. That sure takes all the challenge out of the sport and the fun. Being sinless will not automatically make us perfect in everything we do in heaven. It's not a sin to be ignorant about how to do something. There's nothing wrong with having to learn or improve or hone your skills. People will be at different maturity levels when they arrive in heaven. They will progress from that point. Eternity will be a learning experience as their maturity progresses.

That brings us to a crucial question to some. Will there be sports in heaven? One thing that makes me think there will be sports activities in heaven is that they develop sports and other competitive games in every culture. Even though civilizations had no contact with other cultural groups, they designed games. Does such desire and development have its inception from God's image expressed in us?

If there are sports in heaven, how will that play out when everyone is perfect? Games allow people to develop their abilities and skills in fun ways as they enjoy companionship through competition. Often on earth, sports get out of hand by making the game only about winning rather than displaying skill and sportsmanship. We are disappointed by those who cheat to win. They have little regard for the rules. Some use sports to exert superiority over others. They seek to make others feel inferior or insignificant to build their ego. They fuel their motivation by a 'win at all cost' attitude, and they conclude that winning the game makes them better than others. Sinful attitudes will have no place in heaven.

Just suppose that sports will have a place in heaven. Even though I'm not a die-hard sports fan, I see no reason God would not allow sporting events to be a part of our activities there. People will play sports differently in heaven than on earth. Players will compete because of the joy of the game. Just as players take pleasure in the sport, so will spectators as they delight in the competition and excitement of the game. The competition will not be cutthroat but skilled, friendly, and fun. Players will be concerned with developing their skills and acuteness of their abilities so each can do their best and thus honor God. A person doesn't have to be better than others; they just need to develop their skills to the best of their ability. Competition drives them to excel. Will teams win and lose? Winning is what adds excitement to competition, challenge, and fun. What is the harm of one team winning and the other losing? Each player will seek to play their best with their talents and agility. Their challenge will be to develop strategies and plays to maximize these abilities and efforts. People will not play to exalt themselves but have fun, fellowship with others, and honor our Lord, which will be the purpose of all we do.

Games with different Rules

Do you think players' skills could only be enhanced a limited amount before they've developed to their limit? It's like saying that as professional basketball players get taller, the challenge of making baskets is a lot less difficult. Suppose God changed the playing conditions for the game. God can give us various challenges with each sport. Suppose God changed the gravitational effect on the players or the ball each season. That would change the game. Imagine baseball games played in different intensities of rain or higher winds that God supplied for each game. Envision a soccer game with a uniquely designed field in which three or four teams competed. Each team would defend their goal on one of the sides of the area. Games could be played underwater or in outer space. Okay, I'm grasping for ideas here. I'm not as creative as God is. It would be His department to create obstacles to challenge the playing conditions. Wouldn't that be a hoot to have a season with different gravitational effects on the ball and players alike, or playing the game in a denser atmosphere? Whatever we do, God could certainly have ideas and offer variety to the sport that will give us a challenge. Shouldn't fun be a part of heaven? After all, that is why God gave us emotions.

Fans

Fans will be valuable in heaven too. Perhaps they will do as they do down here. They will cheer their team on, keep stats, and use it as an opportunity to spend time with their friends and meet new friends that have the same interests. Fans will not belittle the players or officials but be encouragers and content to enjoy the sport. It will be customary for the fans to complement their opponents. "Good play you made on our guy." Fans will cheer for their favorite team. "Come on, 16th Century Reformers; you can beat the Wandering Israelites!" Perhaps you will hear about Daniel heading up the Jewish Lions. He, as well as the early Christians, had their experience with the lions. They might play the Jerusalem Warriors, who got their name from the battles they fought over the centuries. What more can you ask for on a team than people who are brave, courageous, and willing to do battle with the best of their ability? Say, we have a pickup game next week. Are you interested in joining us? We'll call ourselves the 21st Century Saints. "Fans, gather around; we have another great game for you."

Game Changers

All involved in sports will be sinless so that no one will lose their temper; none will seek to make anyone feel inferior if they don't win. They won't call each other derogatory names or get into fights over a questionable call. No team will ever feel superior when they win or inferior if they don't. They will play and have fun in the competition and the camaraderie of playing on the team.

What will make playing enjoyable is that people will continue to develop in their understanding, strategies, and skills, and how that relates to honoring God. Sports would not be an end in itself, but provide opportunities to see weaknesses they can improve. Instead of the TV Reporter talking with the athlete after the game about their great plays, he might ask what they discovered about specific needs to improve their attitude, ability, or motivation during the game. In the interview, he may ask the player how it felt to honor the Lord in how he handled that closeout or extraordinary score. Losses will provide people with an opportunity to recognize skills that need development.

105

Why shouldn't we experience as much of a challenge in heaven as we do down here? Imagine playing sports without having to worry about sports injuries anymore.

Will sports be in heaven? Will the sports lover find an opportunity to be involved in competitive sports in heaven? Who knows? If so, there may even be Super-Bowl football there or a Universe Series baseball playoff. Maybe there will be a **P**rofessional **G**olfers **A**ssociation in heaven, but it would accommodate millions of golfers, and the courses may be out of this world. God may put course designers to work designing a whole planet of golf courses. They will create a variety of fairways that will challenge people on every level of ability and strategy to accomplish the impossible shot. No golf course will have the same nature settings. Some will be around wooded areas, lakes, rivers, and ponds. The beauty of the surroundings of each golf course will bring as much delight as the game itself, for it will be a constant reminder of God's greatness and creativity. Are you eager to play? "Fore! I'm playing through. We have a threesome; do you what to join us?"

What value would sports be?

Why would God allow sports in heaven? I'm not saying sporting events will be there, but we can't deny there won't be sports there. Would it be wrong for God to allow us to do those things that are just fun and in which we developed an interest on earth? Is it all right for God to take pleasure in seeing us enjoy certain life activities? Perhaps you can sit in the stands with Jesus and cheer and talk. Just as parents delight in watching their children play, so God will enjoy seeing His children having fun. After all, He put that fun-loving, competitive spirit within them.

The church I pastored in Port Huron had a good softball team and played against competitive teams in the city softball league. One tournament in which we played remains burned in my memory, and all the players as well. We were playing the top team in the league, and there was a friendly rivalry between us. Many of the players have been friends since school days or have known each other for a long time.

The competition was friendly but very intense. Both teams played to win and wanted the victory.

That July afternoon was hot, and everyone was excited about the game. This was one of those games where everyone was ready, emotionally, physically, and mentally. They all played their A-game. As the game proceeded, it went a few innings with no score. Then, midway through the game, we got some players on base and worked one man into home. As we neared the end of the game, the other team loaded the bases and had no outs. The pitchers were at their best. Team members were making exceptional plays. The result was that none of their players made it home by the end of that inning. We held them and won the game, one to nothing. It was a very intense game. Everyone walked away from the game as friends. They still talk about that game and the fun they had to this day. Why can't heaven have entertainment like that for people to be involved in and watch? Playing won't have to curry anyone's ego or provide the venue to prove themselves.

Some may think it is foolish for us to play sports in heaven. However, others would certainly welcome it. Would you like to be on a team? Perhaps learn the latest game so you can meet an entirely new set of friends and even travel to different parts of the universe together. After all, as people play together, they also get to know each other, develop close relationships, and hone each other's skills. That should be the ultimate goal of playing any sport.

Non-competitive sports

Competitive sports are not the only kinds of activities that one can do. Some people also like to hike or bike through the mountains and around lakes. Then some enjoy the challenge of scaling a mountain or exploring caves—some like scuba diving to explore the oceans or lakes or study the fish. Maybe we won't need an airplane to get a bird's eye view of a planet, but we may enjoy soaring high above the planet's surface for an exhilarating perspective.

Some like to explore. Do you think the people of heaven will be limited only to earth, or will all of the universe be open to exploring new worlds and being able to go where no man has gone before? What about exploring the inside of stars and seeing what makes them twinkle? Such exploration would come after much study of the makeup of stars and how they function, act, and react under certain conditions. Jesus, our teacher, may allow the explosion to happen in slow motion so we can see all the details of what transpires when an atom splits. Then He can talk to us about all the forces in play to bring this about.

Don't all of these opportunities open the door to increase our understanding of God and His greatness? With such knowledge gained by personal experience, we will be better able to bring Him glory and honor. God's glory will be our motivation in every pursuit, event, or activity in which we participate while in heaven.

Someone asked what heaven will be like when they arrive. The response by the wise pastor was, "Think of the very best of what you could imagine about heaven. Then realize God will not disappoint you." God does not tell us a lot about heaven. We know that heaven is good, and we will always experience God's presence. For now, all we have is our sanctified imagination to explore what might be the reality and glory of this incredible place. When we get to heaven, God will adjust our ideas with truth, and we will not be disappointed or left wanting. It will be a magnificent experience to express God's image in creative ways in heaven. So, as you think about the next life, don't forget to do something about the way you live out the image of God now. God wants you to value it and take it out for a test drive to see what you can do to grow and become more like God while down here. Eternity for God's child will not disappoint.

Chapter Ten -- Ted's Story

NANCY ENJOYED WALKING the streets of heaven. One day she was strolling through the café section of Heaven with some friends. It was Danny and Fern, whom she met in their first pastoral position.

Nancy paused while talking and suggested, "Let's stop here at the Living Water Café. It's one of my favorite places. I like their pastries and fruit, but the coffee keeps me returning. Have some with me, won't you?" she said with a smile.

Danny, who was always one for a good conversation and food, was eager to stop as soon as Nancy suggested it. It wasn't long until the conversation turned to a familiar topic. It's a topic the residents of heaven never tire of sharing. It was their salvation experience.

Nancy started. "Have you noticed that just about every time you think of your conversion, you find yourself focusing on new aspects of your salvation that you never thought about before you got here? It's exciting to recognize how God was so involved in the details of our salvation and life. God wasn't just involved in the big changes, but also the small nuances of our life."

Fern mentioned that one of the reasons she accepted Christ as Savior was because she was afraid of hell, and she felt some emptiness in her life that would not go away. Danny continued the conversation.

"One of my concerns at that time was a fear of hell also. I remembered that they talked a lot about that fiery place. As much as I tried to put it out of my mind and convince myself that I was good enough, it just kept nagging at me."

"Danny, we sure found Christianity to be a whole lot more than escaping hell," Nancy reminisced. "I loved the closeness of our prayer groups and the new intimacy we found in friendship in the

109

community of believers. On earth, I never imagined how that circle of friends would grow when we got up here."

Danny went on about his conversion experience. "Even though I was a nice guy, and I got along with everyone and didn't cause trouble or hurt people, I knew in my heart something was missing. I learned that my sin offended God. I struggled with sin but didn't realize what it was that was truly bothering me. However, when I got right with God, all my guilt was gone, and I fell in love with God and the purpose He gave me in life."

About that time, Ted, a friend from the church, recognized Nancy, Fern, and Danny and stopped in to chat with them. He was a biker who rode with his gang of friends. Ted was a drug addict and an alcoholic before trusting Christ as Savior. Today was the first time he ran across them since he got here, and they engaged in catch-up conversation for the next hour or so.

"Ted," Nancy said, "We were just talking about our reconciliation experience with God and how He opened our eyes to so many deeper aspects of our salvation that we didn't recognize on earth. It's exciting to see God's big picture of our salvation."

"Nancy, if anyone was a sinner who doesn't deserve to be here, it's me. I could be a real mean dude, and it didn't take much for me to start a fight with someone. I loved my booze, cigarettes, and drugs. There were times I came home so high, I don't even remember how I got there, and sometimes I didn't even know where I was when I got up."

"Ted, we have some time and would love to have you share what you discovered about your salvation as you look back on your life."

"I love doing that, Nancy. By the way, I want to tell you how much you encouraged me in my faith. I also like those smart remarks you threw at me. You weren't afraid to speak the truth to me and seemed to understand me and made it fun to be at church."

110

"That was my pleasure, Ted. I loved giving you a rough time. It usually made my day to have someone with whom to banter."

"As I look back on my life, I am so thankful for the people who prayed for me and continued to be there for me, even when I was persistent in my sinful lifestyle. I can't understand why my mom, wife, and others didn't give up on me. I identified with the Apostle Paul when he said he was the chief of sinners because I sure felt that way about my life. As I look back, I am aware that the reason they didn't give up on me was that they had a love of our Savior in their hearts. That allowed them to love when others would have given up.

"Another thing I have come to appreciate since I got to heaven is how my drugs, smoking, alcohol, and wild actions were the things I used to try to fill the emptiness in my soul. Relationship with God is what makes life fulfilling. My sinful actions were masking my deepest needs, which we all know is intimacy with God. I was looking for pleasure and fulfillment in my sinful actions, but I consistently ran on empty. The emptier I felt, the more I sought to fill it with drugs, alcohol, and good times. All these substitutes for God drove me into more profound despair. It was as if I stepped into quicksand and couldn't get out. The harder I struggled, the deeper I sank.

"Because of my mom, I heard about Jesus and the fact that He died on the cross for me and that by faith, I could receive the gift of eternal life and receive forgiveness. That just seemed too easy, and besides, I knew if I did that, I would surely miss the fun things of life. Then it hit me one day. I'm not having fun living this kind of life. I'm completely miserable. Why am I continuing to travel this dead-end road?

"This is where my hard-nosed attitude was actually beneficial. I immediately decided to quit drugs, drinking, and my wild way of life **TODAY**. I will place my trust in Christ – right now. No one had to plead with me or persuade me to get reconciled with God. Right there in the bar, as I was contemplating whether to take another drink or not, and thinking these very thoughts, God's Spirit opened my eyes to see my need for Jesus. I prayed a simple, sincere prayer. *'Lord, I don't know why the hell I'm living this way. I am a rotten sinner, and I failed you in more ways than I can count. I need Jesus to be my Savior and to deliver me from the hold sin has on my life.'* My prayer wasn't long or fancy, but I honestly gave God my heart in that prayer. Whenever I think of my conversion, I still get emotional about it even here in heaven. God delivered me! At that moment, He showed me how much He loved me. I was actually valuable to Him. The truth that grabbed me with the most significant force, besides forgiveness, was that He wanted me. No one had to tell me. I felt that in my being."

Nancy, Fern, and Danny were all silent for a moment as they rejoiced in their hearts over what God did for Ted.

Danny said, "Let's just take some time to thank Jesus for what He did, and then let's sing about His faithfulness."

With a twinkle in her eye, Nancy looked at Ted and said, "I hope you can sing better now than you could back on earth."

Jokingly he nudged her on the arm, smiled back, and said, "You have to hear the new and improved voice God gave me. I think we're going to sound pretty good together."

Ted smiled, and instead of asking Danny to choose the song, said, "I recently wrote a song about God's loving-kindness in the way he drew me to Himself. Let me sing a couple of stanzas, and you can join in with me. I so love praising God in this way up here."

Suppose you wanted to get right with God

Ted recognized that he wasn't right with God. His sin was a constant reminder of the need he had to address seriously. Ted discerned that his lifestyle was at odds with his Maker in his heart. Indeed, he could claim no favor with God through his goodness. There is only one way a person can come into favor with God.

Every person who wants to go to heaven needs to be reconciled with God to gain His acceptance so they can enter heaven. We have all offended our Creator by our sin. Danny was a nice person, and Ted was a flagrant sinner. Both needed reconciliation with God. The Bible's verdict about the entire human race is that "all have sinned."[69] Sin means that we have missed the mark for God's acceptance. We have disobeyed His laws. We have violated His commandments. We have failed to live up to His standards. Because He is the creator, He has the right to impose His rules on us. Those who want to enter heaven need to accept God's way of how to get right with Him. The Bible, God's Word, explains how we can attain reconciliation with Him.

Having explained that sin separates us from God, I want you to have a realistic understanding of sin. Some think we have to commit many sins to become estranged from God. Adam and Eve violated God's instruction only once and became sinners under the penalty of death. Have you ever told a lie or taken something that didn't belong to you? Have you always spoken the truth or had an impure thought? Jesus said that if a man looks with lust on a woman, he has committed adultery in his heart. Have you always honored God by your actions? If you are guilty of any of these sins, then chances are you have done it more than once and are guilty of more than one of these. Committing any of these sins alienates you from God and requires you to be reconciled with Him.

Our sin causes us to be at odds with God. When two parties are estranged, it takes both to recover the relationship. Consider a husband who cheated on his wife and then realizes the error of his way. If he wants to re-establish his relationship with her, it will take more than a mere desire to reconcile. He could repent and honestly deal with why he went astray and work on wooing his wife back. However, that does not automatically bring about a reconciled relationship. For reconciliation to happen, she also needs to agree to it. Both parties need to want and accept a settlement for reconciliation.

---

[69] Romans 3:10-23, Ecclesiastes 7:20 "Indeed, there is no one on earth who is righteous, no one who does what is right and never sins.

113

The penalty for not being reconciled with God and remaining a sinner, as well as His enemy, means that this person is not acceptable to enter heaven, nor be His friend. All who refuse reconciliation with God will remain His enemy for eternity.[70] There is nothing pleasant about condemnation to hell.[71] Some people don't want to admit that hell is the final judgment for all who are not reconciled with God. To refuse to accept this truth does not change the reality of what God promised.[72]

God made it possible for full acceptance by providing reconciliation for every human being. Jesus accomplished this when He died on the cross. His death was the basis of the total payment for our sin's penalty.[73] In effect, His death made full payment for the sins of every person so God could forgive every offense of all humanity. God has cleared the way for the human race to be acceptable to him from His perspective. *"All this is from God, who reconciled us to himself through Christ and gave us the ministry of reconciliation: that **God was reconciling the world to himself in Christ, not counting people's sins against them.**"*[74] *(Emphasis mine)*

---

70 John 3:18 "Whoever believes in him is not condemned, but whoever does not believe stands condemned already because they have not believed in the name of God's one and only Son."
71 "Then I saw a great white throne and him who was seated on it. The earth and the heavens fled from his presence, and there was no place for them. 12 And I saw the dead, great and small, standing before the throne, and books were opened. Another book was opened, which is the book of life. The dead were judged according to what they had done as recorded in the books. 13 The sea gave up the dead that were in it, and death and Hades gave up the dead that were in them, and each person was judged according to what they had done. 14 Then death and Hades were thrown into the lake of fire. The lake of fire is the second death. 15 Anyone whose name was not found written in the book of life was thrown into the lake of fire." Revelation 20:11-15. "They, too, will drink the wine of God's fury, which has been poured full strength into the cup of his wrath. They will be tormented with burning sulfur in the presence of the holy angels and of the Lamb. And the smoke of their torment will rise forever and ever. There will be no rest day or night for those who worship the beast and its image, or for anyone who receives the mark of its name." Revelation 14:10-11
72 He will punish those who do not know God and do not obey the gospel of our Lord Jesus. They will be punished with everlasting destruction and shut out from the presence of the Lord and from the glory of his might." 2 Thessalonians 1:8-9; "if this is so, then the Lord knows how to rescue the godly from trials and to hold the unrighteous for punishment on the Day of Judgment." 2 Peter 2:9
73 "For God so loved the world that he gave his one and only Son, that whoever believes in him shall not perish but have eternal life." John 3:16
74 2 Corinthians 5:18-19

Notice it says God reconciled the world to himself through Christ. God did everything needed to accept everyone into a right relationship with Him, including you. Jesus made full payment for your sins, so He has provided the means for your acceptance. But something else is required. You wronged Him. You offended God by your sinful actions. The reconciliation process becomes complete when you recognize that you offended God, and now you seek to become right with Him.

To make reconciliation possible, God paid the debt your incurred sin. Because your sin needs forgiveness, Jesus provided the only means for God to forgive your sins, thus gaining acceptance with God. You owed God that debt, but God loved you so much that Jesus paid your debt when He died on the cross.

That brings us around to your responsibility. God did everything from His side to make reconciliation possible. The ball is now in your court for action. If you want to become reconciled with God, accept His payment for your sin and tell Him you want to experience reconciliation with him. How does one do that?

God offers you salvation as a gift. *"For it is by grace you have been saved, through faith—and this is not from yourselves, it is the gift of God, not by works, so that no one can boast."*[75] God wants there to be no question about a person's ability to be reconciled with Him. He offers it as a gift. All that is required to receive a gift is to accept it. Are you willing to receive God's payment for your sin, so you can, in turn, become reconciled with God?

Paul talks about the salvation process in Romans 10:9-10, 13 *"If you declare with your mouth, 'Jesus is Lord,' and believe in your heart that God raised him from the dead, you will be saved. For it is with your heart that you believe and are justified, and it is with your mouth that you profess your faith and are saved."*[76]

---

75 Ephesians 2:8–9
76 Romans 10:9–10 (Justified means you are declared righteous, that is acceptable to God.)

God calls you to respond by faith. In this, you recognize that Jesus is God (Lord) and that when He died, God raised Him from the dead to prove He accepted Jesus' payment for your sin. Notice Paul says that we should confess with our mouth what we believe in our hearts. How do we confess with our mouth?

He makes it simple: *"Everyone who calls on the name of the Lord will be saved."*[77] How do we call on the name of the Lord? We talk to the Lord through prayer. Let me give you a sample prayer that helps you understand how you can address God in requesting your need.

"God, my sin has offended you and broken our relationship. I want to spend eternity with you, and I know that I must become reconciled with you for that to happen. In my heart, I believe Jesus died on the cross and paid the penalty for all my sins. Willingly I admit I wronged you by my sin, and I deserve eternal punishment. I claim reconciliation with you right now because of the death of Jesus on the cross. Thank you for reaching out to me and wanting me as your child and friend. I pray this in Jesus' name. Amen."

Salvation is reconciliation with God. That means that if you prayed for reconciliation with God, you are on good terms with Him right now[78] and are in good standing with Him. You have become not just His friend[79] but also His child[80] , and heaven is now your home.[81]

If this is the first time you have done this or prayed to make sure you are right with God, let me congratulate you and welcome you into

---

77 Romans 10:13

78 "And this is the testimony: God has given us eternal life, and this life is in his Son. Whoever has the Son has life; whoever does not have the Son of God does not have life" 1 John 5:11-12

79 "I no longer call you servants, because a servant does not know his master's business. Instead, I have called you friends, for everything that I learned from my Father I have made known to you" John 15:15

80 "Yet to all who did receive him, to those who believed in his name, he gave the right to become children of God" John 1:12

81 "My Father's house has many rooms; if that were not so, would I have told you that I am going there to prepare a place for you? And if I go and prepare a place for you, I will come back and take you to be with me that you also may be where I am." John 14:2-3.

God's family. You are now an official citizen of heaven and a child of God. Reconciliation with God is now yours. Learn more about your faith by attending a good Bible-believing church weekly. There you can sit under helpful Bible teaching and develop relationships with other Christians. Feed your faith by reading God's word every day[82] to help you understand other aspects of this new relationship with God.

---

[82] Start in the gospel of John, Read the book 2-3 times. Then continue in Romans and read the rest of the New Testament. When reading the Bible, learn to do more than recognize the facts. Ask questions: What does this mean? How can I apply this teaching to my life? What does this teach me about God. Learn to listen to God as you read. God speaks to us through His word.

"Seek the LORD while he may be found; call you on him while he is near: let the wicked forsake his way, and the unrighteous man his thoughts; and let him return to the LORD, and he will have mercy on him; and to our God, for he will abundantly pardon." Isaiah 55:6-7

* * * * * * * * *

The good news is there is nothing we can do that is bad enough to keep us out of Heaven; the bad news is there is nothing we can do good enough to get us into Heaven.

Zig Ziglar

Chapter Eleven -- Get excited about heaven!

FAITH SUSTAINED PETER because he had a clear view of heaven. He tells us that this ought to help us endure life's difficulties.

> *"Praise be to the God and Father of our Lord Jesus Christ! In his great mercy, he has given us new birth into a living hope through the resurrection of Jesus Christ from the dead and into an inheritance that can never perish, spoil, or fade. This inheritance is kept in heaven for you,"*[83]

Peter wants believers to experience motivation by their anticipation of heaven, and he reminds us of the gold mine of wealth waiting for us. What is the *"inheritance that can never perish?"* It is the fact that we are heirs of God and joint-heirs with Christ.[84] Some of that inheritance would include heaven and our eternal home and every needed aspect of our salvation that will make us perfect. It is all the benefits God has in store for us and is waiting for us to enjoy. They are secure by the power of the resurrected Christ. Christian, God wants you to feel confident in the inheritance He has waiting for you in heaven.

If you were going to inherit 20 billion dollars next week, and you knew there was nothing that could keep you from it, would that capture your interests? Would that give you confidence in your financial future? Here God reminds you that your future is secure. Do you think this should be a cause for rejoicing? Is it worth telling others about this great inheritance and letting them know that they can get in on this deal too?

---

[83] 1 Peter 1:3–4

[84] "The Spirit himself testifies with our spirit that we are God's children. Now if we are children, then we are heirs—heirs of God and co-heirs with Christ..." Romans 8:16-17

When I wrote my book on hell, I wanted people to think about two truths. The first is the reality of eternal punishment. The second is how dreadful hell is. I wanted the realism of hell to motivate them to take their relationship with God seriously and to accept God's offer of reconciliation. After all, we need to remind ourselves of the eternal destination of our non-reconciled friends. That should motivate us to talk to our friends about God. Yes, the wrath of God against those in hell should motivate us to action.[85]

One of the purposes of this book on heaven is to motivate God's people to faithfulness. God wants us to be authentic in our devotion to Him[86] and share the gospel message with the non-reconciled.[87] God has an untold blessing waiting for us in heaven that is totally beyond our imagination, and that should provoke us to talk with others about it. In my three-month road trip out west, I saw some of the magnificent beauty of the United States. Since then, I have talked with my friends about the beauty of our country, and I desire to return. I did not expect their response as I talked about my travels. My story inspired them to want to visit various sights I described. Some had considered it before, but my excitement revved up their desire to make the trip themselves.

If we don't take the time to consider some of the specific joys we anticipate in heaven, then chances are we won't get excited about it. Thus, a powerful motivation, which gives us pleasure in talking to others about salvation and heaven, is missing in our impetus.

As I prepared to write this book, and even while writing it, I asked various people about heaven, "What do they think it will be like in heaven?" As we talked about specifics, we got excited about going there. Most people have little idea of what heaven will be like once

---

[85] "But because of your stubbornness and your unrepentant heart, you are storing up wrath against yourself for the day of God's wrath, when his righteous judgment will be revealed." Romans 2:5

[86] "This is how we know we are in him: Whoever claims to live in him must live as Jesus did." 1 John 2:5-6

[87] "My dear friends, if you know people who have wandered off from God's truth, don't write them off. Go after them. Get them back and you will have rescued precious lives from destruction and prevented an epidemic of wandering away from God." James 5:19-20

they arrive. Often, they aren't too enthusiastic about heaven, except they know they are going there, and it will be magnificent. Why do I say that? Think about it. How often do you hear Christians being excited when talking about heaven? Why are they so quiet about this magnificent place?

Christians need to talk with non-believers about heaven. Why should non-Christians get excited about heaven if the greatness of this place does not energize the Christians? My purpose for this book is to give you thinking points to become more enthusiastic about heaven and going there. It is our joyful anticipation about the realities of heaven and should enliven our conversation for both believers and non-believers. God openly presents both truths and ideas about heaven. We must also extrapolate some facts about heaven from the teachings of Scripture. I sought to do that with the concepts I present in this book.

1 Corinthians says, "*No mind has conceived the things God has prepared for those who love him.*"[88] Even though I offered some interesting things that may happen in heaven, one thing is for sure, what is in heaven is more exciting and fabulous than the things we can imagine. I have shared some possible ideas of how we may experience the continual development of the image of God when we arrive in heaven. I based my approach on my decades of Bible study from which I gleaned truths that I sought to apply to life in heaven. I don't know of any other way to come to an understanding of what we will do in heaven except to wait until we get there.

It has been exhilarating to share my thoughts with people about heaven. Almost without exception, every Christian I talked with saw the real possibilities of this line of thinking. The result was that they became more excited about heaven. I was talking with my friend Kim, whose wife is also Kim. He said he married her so he wouldn't forget his name. Talking about heaven caused our excitement to increase. What will it be like to live there? The more we talked, the more enthusiastic we got, and new ideas kept coming to mind. We both became more eager to get to heaven. When was the last time you got

---

[88] 1 Corinthians 2:9

someone excited about heaven? What fear causes you not to talk about heaven? I would venture to say that you are not thinking about heaven much, and you don't know what to think about it. If you don't have any specific ideas that motivate your imagination to think about heaven, then it's hard to be excited about it. When you don't understand heaven's reality, then you settle for an inferior view of your eternal home. It's a lovely place, but I don't know what to get excited about it.

I hope this book helps you think a little more realistically, so you have greater anticipation in your heart and a renewed excitement about heaven that motivates you to talk with others about it. Start conversations by asking people what they think heaven will be like, and then share your ideas or the ideas you read in this book. See where it takes you in your conversation with your friends or even strangers. You will find that your excitement will attract others to this topic.

Thoughts of heaven invaded my mind as I wrote this book. One of the unexpected blessings I received while writing on this topic was that for several weeks when I went to church to worship or during Scripture reading, further ideas would flood my mind about heaven. The last chapter came to me in a worship service I attended in Holland, Michigan. The idea was so powerful that I scrapped my final chapter and rewrote it that week. I hope you enjoy it. What I'm saying is that while I was engaging my mind on heaven so intently, God opened my understanding to other truths. We have experienced new knowledge in different ways in our life. When we go through grief or hardship, verses open up, and we gain new meaning and understanding we never considered before. It's time for you to concentrate on heaven and see what God opens up to you.

As you develop your concept of heaven, you will be thrilled anew about being with God and anticipate the things He has in store for you. Your genuine excitement may easily attract others. Your new attitude may even open the door for you to talk to them about their need for reconciliation with God. The best part of communicating with them is seeing them decide to become a citizen of heaven. They will then be your friend forever. Don't go to heaven alone. Take someone with you.

Entice them to heaven with God's love story and the exciting life awaiting them when they choose to become a member of God's family.

~~~~~~~~~~~~~~~~~~~~~~~~~~~~~~~~~

What no eye has seen, what no ear has heard,
and what no human mind has conceived"—
the things God has prepared for those who love him—
these are the things God has revealed to us by his Spirit.
The Spirit searches all things, even the deep things of
God. For who knows a person's thoughts except their own
spirit within them? In the same way, no one knows the
thoughts of God except the Spirit of God. What we have
received is not the spirit of the world, but the Spirit who is
from God, so that we may understand what God has freely
given us. This is what we speak, not in words taught us by
human wisdom but in words taught by the Spirit, explaining
spiritual realities with Spirit-taught words.
1 Corinthians 2:9-13 NIV

"You know, eternal life does not start when we go to heaven. It starts the moment you reach out to Jesus. He never turns His back on anyone. And He is waiting for you."

Corrie Ten Boom

"The most thrilling thing about heaven is that Jesus Christ will be there. I will see Him face to face. Jesus Christ will meet us at the end of life's journey."

Billy Graham

"The fact that our heart yearns for something Earth can't supply is proof that Heaven must be our home."

C. S. Lewis

Chapter Twelve -- Prelude to Eternity

The End - The Beginning

THE BOOK OF REVELATION brings us to the finale of this earth. All the events described have transpired, including seven years of tribulation on planet earth, in which the unredeemed sinners experience God's wrath[89] designed to wake them up to their need for repentance.[90] During this time, Satan focuses His wrath on Israel and seeks to destroy them.[91] The tribulation culminates with the battle of Armageddon.[92]

Following that great battle, Jesus sets up His earthly Kingdom and takes away Satan's influence by locking him away for 1,000-years.[93] Peace reigns on earth during His 1,000-year reign. The kingdom age concludes with Satan's final revolt, after which an angel throws him into the lake of fire. What follows is the judgment of all unsaved humanity in which Jesus judges them for their sins and sentences them to the home they chose for eternity, which is the lake of fire. God then creates a new heaven and earth and provides an eternal home for those who are His.

Not all believers agree about the order of these events. Read Revelation 19-22 to see the end of God's program for the earth. I am presenting the chronological details. The stage is now set for the beginning of eternity for all believers. I said all of this to say, now let eternity begin for God's people.

---

[89] Revelation 6:16-17; 14:18-20
[90] Revelation 9:20-21
[91] Revelation 12:13-17, Revelation 9:20-21
[92] Revelation 19:11-21
[93] Revelation 20-21:3 spells out most of what is said in this paragraph

I think God likes celebrations. He wants us to mark beginnings with special recognitions. Think of all the feasts and festivals of the Old Testament. Then there are communions and baptisms in the New Testament. The book of Revelation has great worship responses when significant events take place. Revelation 4-5 describes when God declares that He is now ready to take back the world for Himself. In chapter four, God claims His right to regain control of the world because of His authority as the Creator.[94] In chapter five, Jesus, the Lamb of God, claims His right over humanity because of His work as Redeemer, the only Savior of humanity.[95] There are several more worship scenes for various reasons throughout the rest of the book.

The worship scene I talk about in this chapter is not in the book of Revelation. It takes place beyond the focus of Revelation. This chapter visits the opening worship session that brings everyone together. I want to think of it as a combination of a victory celebration and a kick-off rally for eternity. Allow me to help you see a possible way this celebration may occur—picture a great gathering in heaven in your mind's eye. Now allow me to paint a picture of the opening ceremony that takes us into eternity as God welcomes us and allows us to worship Him with unrestrained emotion, understanding, and love.

Anticipating the event

The crowds are getting more substantial, and even though there is lots of room, we are bumping into each other. No one is getting irritated or upset by the crowds. Even though millions of people are heading to the same destination, everyone is courteous, cheerful, and upbeat. There is an air of excitement and expectancy among each one. After all, God is gathering all the saints and angels together for a one-of-a-kind praise fest. We've been talking about it for months, and everyone is wondering what God has in store. He said that even though there would be many more praise festivals on His schedule, this one is unique. Everyone wants to know what the creator has in mind for this

---

[94] Revelation 4:11
[95] Revelation 5:6, 9-10

prodigious festive event. Our talk about this celebration has been non-stop.

Spirits are running high because many just recently received their resurrection bodies and are experiencing that new freedom in this sin-free environment. Some were mentally disabled on earth and could not think properly, speak clearly, or use all their motor skills in the way God intended. Many were paralyzed, lost a limb, or could not see or hear, and they are all perfectly healed and fully functional. Those who had limited mental capacities could think clearly and creatively because they are now whole. It was so neat to watch some of them jump, run, and do cartwheels as people arrived. Those who had vocal impediments talked a mile a minute, and some sang everywhere they went. They just loved their new freedom to express themselves.

Those are not the only kinds of impediments from which people experienced release. There were shouts of joy and celebration from those who battled addictions, those who struggled with fear, depression, and inferiority. Every spiritual and emotional struggle was now gone, and all of us experienced a refreshing freedom in our newly transformed bodies. Their strong desire to show appreciation to God for what Jesus did for them has not had the proper opportunity for full expression yet.

Down on earth, we would say there is electricity in the air. Since the announcement of the praise fest, excitement has been building. Emotions are running high. Like a racehorse ready to run as soon as the gate springs open, every muscle in our bodies is twitching to get started to offer honor and praise to God because of all He did for us. We just cannot withhold our expression of appreciation much longer — all of us are eagerly anticipating this grand event. Such a single focused gathering of saints to praise God has not happened yet, because not all the family was yet home.

At times, I could not contain myself and would break into song as we walked toward the gathering place. Many of those who were an essential part of my life were with me. My relationship with earthly family and friends continued in heaven. We found ourselves singing some of our old favorite worship songs, as well as making up a few as we walked.

The closer we came to the event arena, the more difficult it was to contain ourselves. The gathering place was vast to accommodate all the saints, as well as the millions of angels. On earth, such a gathering could not happen because most of the audience would be too far away to feel a part of the celebration. However, this is God's event, and He has this one covered. Everyone will fully feel a part of this event because God designed it, so you don't have to be close to see, hear, and enjoy this occasion. God showed His creativity in providing a single gathering place for all the citizens of heaven. He just called it the Event Center. Everyone can see and participate without having to look around someone's head. I am glad I do not have to figure out how God can make more than 20 billion people feel close to this event. That shows you how innovative our God is. Nothing is too hard for Him.

There were no clogged lines at the entrances, but every aspect of the event moved smoothly as we entered quickly and disseminated to our seats. Some people were late, even here in heaven. You know who they are. They are the ones who always came late to events on earth. They still possessed that trait in heaven. I remember an old friend, Linda, who thought that if the service started at 7:00, that's the time she should leave home to get there. I guess they brought that different drummer to which they always marched.

The excitement has not subsided since we got to our seats; in fact, it's just been intensifying. People are eager to express their appreciation as a group. Starting time is upon us, and everyone is in place. In the center, there was a raised platform with beautiful thrones encircled with a rainbow of lights.

"That has to be where God will present Himself to us. It is so beautiful and awe-inspiring for our God, who is supreme." I thought.

Praise Fest

Suddenly, there was movement in the center stage area. Everyone immediately went silent. With heightened expectations, the sudden quietness was almost deafening. People watched the stage area intently, with anticipation. Then it began. It started with the entrance of a delegation of high-ranking angels. Those who followed the angels were saints clothed in white robes. They were elders of Israel and the Church. These faithfully served the Lord in unique capacities during their life. We honored them for devotedly serving the Lord and guiding God's people through their various times of need. Even though we didn't recognize these saints right away, their identity became apparent. The Holy Spirit introduced them to us in our minds as He explained their service to God. We all knew the kind of commitment and devotion leaders need to serve the Lord. God used them to impact His people and the world significantly. The applause rang out for an appropriate time. Then, almost as on cue, quieted as quickly as it began. We knew this time was not about them right now, but the One we anticipated.

No one expected the unusual entrance God made. It was not pomp and ceremony but a sudden appearance on center stage. He appeared sitting on a throne, similar to His presentation in Revelation 4:3, "*And the one who sat there had the appearance of jasper and ruby. A rainbow that shone like an emerald encircled the throne.*" It's not that God needed a throne with its splendor. He does not need anything to distinguish His glory or authority. When God appeared in His glory, we were all in awe, and everyone went quiet out of respect. Then everyone, as if on cue, bowed in worship and adoration.

Our hearts were so full of love for God; we had to honor Him. We had to! Lest the stones cry out, our voices needed to praise God. Our voices sounded as we expressed our love and admiration for Him. Instinctively, every one of us knew what to sing, and the praise started and would not stop. Some of the newer people had little experience with their new voice. Those who lacked singing ability on earth quickly discovered that they could sing to new heights of expression. Those who could sing realized their improved ability. The sopranos sang higher, clearer, and enunciated with absolute clarity. The basses sang lower, the altos carried their part and harmonized with the sopranos, as did the baritones with the tenors. Each found that they could fully express their hearts through their singing. You ought to hear them harmonize. The quality of their song had no comparison to anything we ever heard on earth. No one's voice grew weak from overuse or experienced tiredness. They were able to sing with uninhibited passion. They expressed levels in their singing they never thought possible. Some embellished the worship with their counter melodies.

Within every section, singers and instrumentalists were playing their hearts out. Those who loved to play on earth were doing the accompanying. Those who played an instrument in school but never touched it since were having the time of their life. There were guitars, keyboards, organs, percussion instruments, horns, and woodwinds. They were playing every musical instrument imaginable. Do you know what else was neat about this? Not one person hit a wrong note but played their instrument skillfully. Chuck[96] was heading up a section of trumpets, and you could hear and feel his excitement as he played. Two of my grandchildren, Christian and Trinity, played with a group of sax players. The Tennants were all on their string instruments. No one needed sheet music for each knew what to play. The Holy Spirit enabled each to express their heart and soul for this event fully.

Sixteen Choirs

Then something very remarkable happened. The seating of the vast audience moved, dividing the gathering into 16 different choirs. Every one of them started to sing a new song they had never before heard as the Spirit composed various songs for each choir that expressed the joy of their redemption and praise to God. They sang with an animated expression that flowed from them so naturally. Each choir is now exalting the greatness of God in their specific way.

---

[96] In this chapter, I use names of people I know. It is my way of honoring them and making heaven more personal. Their friends will recognize who they are. Identity of these people is not needful for the reader to know in order to understand the context. Whose name might you insert in some of these places?

One declared **God's extraordinary grace** in dealing with humanity, even though we deserved no favor from Him at all. Another proclaimed the **mercy of God's way** among errant people. Two different choirs were extolling various aspects of the **boundless love of God** and its expressions through the ages. A strong men's section sang about the **passion of our Lord Jesus**. Their focus was on what He endured as He experienced the horrors of the cross. They extolled His sacrifice for sin in providing redemption. The women's section sang of the **work of the Holy Spirit** in the lives of His people, how He empowered them and patiently worked with them, guiding, teaching, instructing, empowering, and leading them.

From the left section, another group sang His praises of **how He not only drew them into salvation** but also sought to draw the lost to Him. Some accepted, but many more rejected the gospel and are now in hell. Another group extolled the **glory of God's Word** as they focused on how it provided them the means of understanding God and how to live. Those who remained unmarried sang about the **sustaining power of God** and the way He honored His promises among those who chose to believe and trust Him. A [97]children's choir sang about the **personal relationship God designed for His people** to enjoy Him and the great love He has for them. Pastors and missionaries sang about the **privilege they had to serve others, preach, and teach the Word of God**. In that group, I saw men I worked with in ministry over the years singing together, Bill, Gene, Vince, Marty, Arnold, Jessie, and Dan. They emphasized the joy from their extended time studying God's Word and the opportunity of serving and leading God's people.

From the opposite side of the throne, those who had been drunkards, addicts, criminals, prostitutes, and the imprisoned sang about the blessings of **God's gracious salvation**, noting especially forgiveness of sins and gaining a life-changing purpose. The judges, lawyers, and law keepers of earth sang about **God's justice and care of mistreated** and abused people. I was delighted to recognize some of

---

[97] No, I don't know if children will still be children in heaven. My tendency is to think that children, who died on earth won't remain children in heaven. That is my guess. Because there is no biblical teaching on this topic, no one really knows.

my lawyer friends, Kel, Will, John, and Tom, were singing together. They were having the time of their lives praising God. A section of doctors, nurses, and caregivers joined in singing about **God's healing power**, His compassion on the sick, and the privilege of helping people God loved.

Then a choir off to my right joyfully sang of the **benefits of the saving work of God**, the joy of being a new creation, and the full acceptance into God's family. Former skeptics made up the last choir and sang about **God's patience in wooing them to Himself** and the wisdom of God and His grand design of the world.

Each group was singing a different song simultaneously, blending flawlessly, yet everyone could hear what the other groups were singing. Their spirits meshed, which enhanced their expression of praise to God. Then came the refrain at precisely the same time, and each group blended in a unique harmonic vocalization as no one had ever heard. This refrain extolled God's worthiness and greatness. No one could understand how they could do this and still follow what was going on all around them. This new existence is beyond all of our expectations. Those who could not carry a tune on earth found that they could now express their heart through their voices. They rejoiced in this opportunity to be able to sing with such expression.

We had another experience as we raised our voices in praise to God. It was our total freedom of expression. Whereas we would stammer or hem and haw in getting out our thoughts down here, there was complete freedom to express ourselves in heaven. The freedom from guilt and the presence of sin set us completely free. We didn't realize how sin held us in bondage until we got here. Now each of us felt the freedom from sin's bondage. We praise God that it is gone forever!

No one experienced such fantastic praise time before. There was no set order. No pre-planned songs, chants, or praise choruses. Out of the unorganized crowds came the most orderly and spontaneous praise ever heard. The Holy Spirit was able to direct all of us because of the absence of self and sin.

I have no idea how long this went on; it could have been hours or days. It was an extremely enjoyable time proclaiming the greatness of our God. As this part of the praise fest concluded, I thought it was the end, for it was undoubtedly one of the best praise times I ever experienced or heard. I felt that anything after this would undoubtedly be anti-climactic.

God the Creator

Then something moved, and our attention refocused. It took me a moment, but soon I recognized the scene around the throne. The scene described in Revelation 4 speaks of the time when it declares God has the right to take over the earth because He is the Creator. That is significant because creation affirms God's glory, power, and authority. It was a majestic, soul-gripping scene. In the act of both worship and submission, we saw the elders bow down to honor God.

> They lay their crowns before the throne and say:
> "You are worthy, our Lord and God,
> to receive glory and honor and power,
> for you created all things,
> and by your will, they were created and have their being"[98]
> "Great and marvelous are your deeds, Lord God Almighty.
>
> Just and true are your ways; who will not fear you, Lord,
> and bring glory to your name? For you alone are holy.
> All nations… come and worship before you,
> for your righteous acts have been revealed."[99]
> "Hallelujah! For our Lord God Almighty reigns.
> Let us rejoice and be glad and give him glory!" [100]

Yes! God is the great Creator. His power, creativity, attention to detail, and imagination are far beyond our wildest dreams. We have the

---

[98] Revelation 4:10–11
[99] Revelation 15:3–4
[100] Relation 19:6–7

rest of eternity to explore His genius in a myriad of ways through which He shows His wisdom and power in creation.

As soon as that segment of praise concluded, something entirely unexpected appeared. There descended a holographic globe of the earth hovering above God, and it was huge. It was large enough for all to see in its entirety. I would estimate that its diameter was ten miles. Suddenly, we found ourselves seated around that globe without realizing our movement. In real-time motion, the creation of the heavens and the earth started taking place before our very eyes. The display of God bringing about His creation was in brilliant detail and color. The scene moved quickly from one event of His creation to another.

First, the world was covered by water; then, the seas and land separated. After that, we watched the vegetation on the earth grow to full maturity. He told us there were over 391,000 kinds of plants, and most were flowering. He spread more than 60,000 species of trees over the earth. We saw every type of plant, tree, and vegetation come into being. Everything grew quickly into maturity, and we seemed to understand the creative detail of some of these plants. God didn't want to reveal everything, but He wanted to grab our interest. We all became aware that this is how rapidly creation occurred. We were beholding an actual replay of creation.[101] We recognized some of the plants immediately, for they were a part of our life. Others were brand new to us scattered around the world.

In the next day's events, we saw the sun come into being. Appearing next was the moon and stars. They were God's nightlights. The stars made their appearance by bursting out like fireworks on a Fourth of July celebration. The twinkling starry lights made the night beautiful; after all, he made more than one billion trillion stars. He reminded us that He named them all according to their characteristics.

Following that, the water life started to come alive. God created every kind of fish, and they started teeming and swimming through the

---

[101] Genesis 1

waters. There were more than 18,000 species of freshwater fish, followed by 20,000 types of salt-water fish and 210,000 marine life forms. Their brilliant colors and detail awed every one of us. I don't know how our minds comprehended seeing the details of every fish and remembering them all. More happened on that day. God drew our attention from the water to the air and brought in his feathered air force. Oh, what magnificent creatures we saw with their unique beauty. Feathers of all colors adorned the birds. Each had its different ability, purpose, and style of flight. God directed them to put on an air show for us, displaying their flying proficiency and uniqueness. There were over 10,000 varieties of birds on display. He featured the different nesting habits of each as kind of a sideshow. This part of the demonstration displayed His unique design ability. He then made sure we saw His vast assortment of small creatures. After all, he made ten million different kinds of insects, which had an essential duty. Even though we called them pests on earth, God had an explicit and particular purpose for them all.

Land animals were next on the scene. Each animal displayed various aspects of God's creativity in the way they looked and how they moved, as well as their purpose. He had the animals enter like a circus parade and marched them around the globe to display each species. There were over 8.5 million species of animals, which included every variation of each kind. Pet owners delighted at the vast display of all the types of cats or dogs. Their hearts skipped a beat when they saw their favorite. God showed us each of the animal kinds. The dog family included every type of canine, from the Chihuahua to the Great Dane and the wolf to the fox. Through breeding, God allowed each kind to transform into different types of the dog family. Each came out jumping, playing, running, and even doing flips as they displayed their uniqueness. They were not just performing for us, but their creator.

The domestic animals had a particular section. These are the ones designed to help feed humanity and do our heavy work, as well as be companions. Those animals considered wild had their place in the parade. God displayed large and small animals together. We saw some of the petite animals playfully riding on the large ones. The procession marched off into the four quadrants of the world.

While intently watching this parade, we abruptly realized that God was actually creating them as they walked on the scene. He did this to display His infinite power and ability. Creating seemed like a simple task to God that demonstrated incredible designs and purpose. God wanted us to experience His glory in the display of His astonishing ability. He displayed the animals we were familiar with and those that became extinct because of man's carelessness, cruelty, or selfishness.

Some of us watched the parade of animals and were amazed because we recognized God's glory. Others watched with a completely different interest because they could hardly wait to get out among them and observe them and learn as much about them and God's magnificent design as possible. Some just wanted to claim one as a pet.

The final act of creation was humanity. Humans are the crown jewel of His creation because we bear His image. In the final scene, we notice the face of God after He finished His creation. God's smile of satisfaction captivated our attention. Most of us never gave it a moments' thought about how God felt as he created everything until we saw his smile. It grabbed our hearts. He was so delighted in humanity. You could tell He was in love with humans. When He finished creating Adam and Eve, the expression of great delight on His face is something we will never forget. He had the unashamed excitement of a child who just did something fun. He leaned back and looked at Adam and Eve, and with a smile of absolute satisfaction, said, *"This is very good."* God's love for humanity has not dissipated over the centuries.

He then turned his attention from Adam as he surveyed all of us. That same smile of delight shone on His face as He looked into each of our faces. He had eye-to-eye contact with every one of us, and we all realized in our hearts that we were the reason He was smiling. His smile showed us that He was our proud Daddy. The reality of His love penetrated our hearts and souls in such a powerful and unforgettable manner. We knew His love would never falter but would only become more evident in the eons to come.

Everyone was amazed as we recognized that God was replaying the actual creation of the world. He wanted us to know not only that He created the world but also how quickly He brought everything into being. He wanted us to see Him create the world and have that image burned into our memories, to know our origin.

God thoughtfully went on and said, "I want you all to understand why this is important to me. That should then make it very important to you. Because you are my creation, you belong to me. As you know, the world belonged to me, and Satan took it to try to prove that his way of running the world without me could work.[102] I gave him more than 6,000 years to prove his point. When his time was up, I claimed my authority, as the creator, to regain the earth because it belongs to me.[103] I am reminding you through this display of creation that you are mine because I created you. You belong to me, not as my slaves, but as my children, my friends that I love."

"When you recognize me as Creator, you then realize that because I made you, that I also understand you. I know what makes you tick. Since you got here, you have noticed that you retain much of your earthly personality. There is no essence of sin left in your being, and only the positive traits remain in you. I'm glad you value the way I made you, and you will continue to enjoy the ramifications of your personality and our relationship with you here in heaven. I placed my image in you, so I know what you need and what will satisfy you. I know what will bring you pleasure and joy in your life. Just as these features are important to me, I know how important they are to you. I want you to understand that developing my image in you is how I will work with you and reveal myself to you as we live together as friends through eternity."

God used a great way to tie the creation and His purpose of our existence together. I like the fact that He emphasized our purpose clearly. We belong to God, and He is our God.[104]

---

[102] Isaiah 14:12-14
[103] Revelation 4
[104] Revelation 21:3

There wasn't applause after what God communicated to us. Instead, our spontaneous praise declared God's magnificent work as the creator. We expressed our worship in song. One section sang about the beauty and variety of flowers. Another group sang an upbeat song about playful baby animals and their antics. There was an airy melodic song about the beauty of sea creatures and their brilliant colors. Children sang about caring dogs and cats like the ones they enjoyed on earth. Outdoor splendor was the theme of another section as they declared the majestic beauty of the mountains and the calming waterfalls and colorful flowers and autumn forests. In a grand finale, we sang about the creation of man and God's lavish grace He displayed to us, as well as the value He placed on us. It was such a precious time of praising God for His creation.

The presentation of creation was magnificent. We honored and worshipped God as Creator. His handiwork was specular. God's power and wisdom thoroughly thrilled us. The exhibition of God's glory, power, and wisdom will never leave our thoughts. Everyone understood God's purpose for the creation display, and it endeared us even more to Him.

Jesus the Redeemer

Without saying anything further, Jesus presented Himself to us seated on His throne. I shall never forget the immediate response by every person there. We all fell to our knees and began to thank and worship Him for His great sacrifice that accomplished redemption and reconciled us to God. Our time of thanksgiving turned into praise and adoration, focusing on His willingness to lay down His life for us and the display of His great love. We used the very words written in Revelation.

"You are worthy because you were slain,
and with your blood, you purchased for God persons
from every tribe and language and people and nation.
"Salvation belongs to you God, who sits on the throne,
and to the Lamb
Worthy are you, Lord Jesus, for you were slain.

138

"To you be praise and honor and glory and power, forever and ever!"

We continued with what Paul declared in Philippians 2.

> "Therefore God exalted you to the highest place and gave you the name
> that is above every name, that at your name, Jesus, every knee should
> bow, in heaven and on earth and under the earth, and every tongue
> acknowledge that You are Lord, to the glory of God the Father."[105]

Jesus then stood, and everyone quieted immediately. Without
saying a word, He raised His hand to call our attention to the next part
of the presentation. It was His real-life holographic presentation of His
arrest, trial, crucifixion, burial, and resurrection. The uniqueness of this
presentation was that we not only saw what happened to Him, but He
also allowed us to listen in on His thoughts as the events played out.
Not only did we hear what he was thinking during these events, but we
also felt His abandonment, betrayal, the hurts of His unjust accusation,
as He experienced the rejection of His people and the unmerciful
beating by the Romans. Jesus also allowed us to experience bits of the
suffering He faced that day at the hands of His Father.[106] *The Father
laid on Him the iniquity of us all." "It pleased the Lord to bruise him."*

Throughout the whole presentation, Jesus allowed us to listen in on
His thoughts, and the Father freely shared His perspective too. Jesus
was suffering while His Father watched what His Son was enduring
with total empathy. The significant events happened in real-time. We
were all mesmerized as we drank in every word and felt their heart and
concern. Father God shared with great emotion how crushed His heart
was as Jesus not only suffered at the hands of man but also as He had to
crush Jesus unmercifully for the punishment of our sins. We heard and

---

[105] Philippians 2:6–11

[106] "He was oppressed and afflicted, yet he did not open his mouth; he was led like a lamb to the
slaughter, and as a sheep before its shearers is silent, so he did not open his mouth. By
oppression and judgment, he was taken away. Yet who of his generation protested? For he
was cut off from the land of the living; for the transgression of my people he was punished.
He was assigned a grave with the wicked and with the rich in his death, though he had done
no violence, nor was any deceit in his mouth. Yet it was the LORD's will to crush him and
cause him to suffer, and though the LORD makes his life an offering for sin…" Isaiah 53:7-
10 NIV

felt the heart of God, and the passion they both had for the redemption of sinful man, and how His Son's suffering broke the Father's heart. Every one of us empathized with Him. As God was expressing His heart, our hearts moved with the most profound empathy. After His arrest and during His trial, we saw His response to Peter's denial. None of us condemned Peter because we all realized that we, too, denied our Lord in so many ways during our life. Then there was that highly emotional beating He suffered from the soldiers, the anguish inflicted on His journey to the cross, the pain as they nailed Him to the cross, the insults from His accusers, and what He had to endure to pay for our sins. We silently watched as he hung there, suffering on our behalf.

No one was prepared for what was about to happen. As we watched Jesus suffering for our sins on that cross, suddenly, each of us became aware of every one of our sins and the agony it was bringing on our Savior. It wasn't just our significant sins, but in the space of a few moments, God made us aware of every one of our failures, sins, and disobedience. However, that was not all. Our sins moved from our invisible thoughts to a visible display above each of our heads. The best way I can describe it is like a text balloon hovering above each person's head. Listed inside was every single one of our sins. Suddenly there was movement. We did not know what it was at first, but as we gathered our thoughts, we recognized what it was. It was the Father reaching out to every one of us and gathering our sins into one giant mass. What happened next was eye opening to each of us.

The Father then crushed Jesus with the weight of our sins.[107] As soon as He did that, Jesus cried out in heart-wrenching agony. Grief immediately overwhelmed our hearts as we, too, experienced anguish in our innermost being. We could not hold our emotions in, for we felt the pain of His suffering for our sins. Every one of us empathized with His anguish for us. The torture He was experiencing was unlike anything any person ever endured. His torment was inexpressible. As terrible as it was, yet it was so beautiful. He was doing this because He loved us, and we felt His love in the depth of our being.

---

[107] Isaiah 53:6. The above passage of verses 7-10 fit here also.

At that moment, Jesus cried out in a loud agonizing scream, *My God, my God. Why have you forsaken me?* Never had either the Father or Son experienced any separation in their relationship. Both felt an emptiness that was unfathomable and foreign to them. The Father shared how He had to turn His back on the Son, for He could not look on sin. He crushed Him and poured out His full wrath upon Him unmercifully and unrelentingly. How could He do that? How could Jesus take it? Yet, we all knew. It was because the innocent had to suffer for the guilty[108] , and our sins were reprehensible and totally unacceptable to a holy God. We stood there stunned at the agony we heard, not just in His groans and the pain we saw on His face, but also as He allowed us to experience a taste of the agony of His soul as He suffered. His eyes spoke volumes about His agonizing pain as He looked at each of us. It became evident why Jesus said in the garden, *"Father, if it be your will, let this cup pass from me."*[109] We now understood more fully how terrible our sin was to God...to our Savior...to our Friend who willingly died for us.

While we were focusing on His suffering, something extraordinary happened. God was allowing us to tune into the thoughts of Jesus. He was not concentrating on His anguish but had both sorrow and joy as names were racing through his mind. Each name was cited so fast we could only comprehend some names here and there, and they meant nothing to most of us. Every name, however, was significant to Jesus because he knew them. For the longest time, at the mention of each name, it brought a weight of sadness and sorrow over Jesus. The list went on for over an hour, and then his whole demeanor changed. His suffering did not let up, but you could sense the joy in Jesus' mind at the hearing of these names. It was then that the Holy Spirit opened our understanding. Those names that brought sadness were the ones who would reject His provision of salvation and spend eternity in the lake of fire. Those names that brought joy were the ones who would receive reconciliation and enter a relationship with God.[110] The name of every

---

[108] 2 Corinthians 5:21 "God made him who had no sin to be sin for us, so that in him we might become the righteousness of God."

[109] Matthew 26:42 "My Father, if it is not possible for this cup to be taken away unless I drink it, may your will be done."

[110] Hebrews 12:2 (NIV) "...fixing our eyes on Jesus, the pioneer and perfecter of faith. For the

person passed through His mind during that time of suffering. His agony came out of His love for both those who would accept or reject Him.

While experiencing the heart and mind of Jesus, every one of us was stone cold sober. How could we have joy during His agony? It was as if our hearts went dark. Each one experienced the hurt emotionally that we caused Jesus as He was paying for our sins. We watched Him as we internalized what He endured during those three hours of suffering. Jesus then cried out, *"It is finished!"* Immediately His pain ceased. Our souls were again at peace. Then we watched as they took Jesus from the cross and placed Him in the cold tomb. No one was stirring. You could hear a pin drop as time passed, and we contemplated what this meant to us personally. During the next several hours, we watched the tomb from outside. God wanted to give us time for the reality of what happened to Jesus to sink in. On the morning of the third day, an angel took us inside to see Him lying dead on the hewn stone ledge. Jesus, the eternal God, the source of all life, lay dead. He experienced the ultimate punishment to redeem us. However, death could not hold Him. Suddenly a flash of light that was so brilliant and intense that it blinded us briefly came from the tomb! The stone rolled away! Jesus victoriously rose to life and exited the sepulcher triumphantly! He defeated death… **He was ALIVE!**

Watching the scene awakened anew the feeling of that moment when the angels saw Jesus rise from the dead. Without any prompting, they rejoiced and celebrated as they did back then. They could not hold themselves back because of the exuberance that filled their heart. Their rejoicing was totally unrestrained as it was back on that day. Oh, how they loved their Lord!

We followed Jesus through His full passion, just as it happened. We more fully understood our appalling sinfulness and the suffering He endured because of our disobedience. This presentation opened our eyes to a fuller understanding of the cost of our rebellion. He endeared

---

joy set before him he endured the cross, scorning its shame, and sat down at the right hand of the throne of God."

our hearts to Him because we entered His suffering by hearing His thoughts and feeling His pain that He endured for us. We knew more fully the enormous cost of our sin to God, and none of us ever wanted to hurt God like that again.

In awe of Jesus' resurrection, what surprised me is that every one of us was still aware of our personal sin that caused the death and suffering of Christ. I shall never forget our reaction to the whole crucifixion scene. No one shed a tear, for we knew He removed our guilt because of that event. His death purchased for us complete and total forgiveness. God's goal was not for us to experience guilt but always to remember the high cost of our sin to Him. God wanted us to know that He valued a relationship with us so much that He was willing to make complete and total payment for our sin by laying down His life. Every one of us spontaneously responded in heartfelt appreciation, expressing thanks from the depths of our hearts. We erupted into spontaneous worship. We glorified Jesus, our Savior, for His finished work of redemption on the cross. We held nothing back as we sang and praised Him

I expected everyone to sing for at least the next few hours, but the Spirit quieted us after the first praise song. Our attention turned to a woman named Christy, who then sang a solo. Her words rang out in a crystal-clear voice. This soprano soloist sang the first stanza. Before we could respond, the next soloist, who was in the section across from us, sang the second stanza. He was a tenor. Three men standing next to him then joined him. The quartet sang the third verse. The meaning of the song burned into the soul of every one of us. It reminds us of our Savior's love and great sacrifice expressed through His death. The selected hymn was not a new one, but an old hymn, which declared the suffering of Christ on the cross and what it provided for us in such a luxurious way. It was Charles Wesley's hymn, "And Can it be?"

> And can it be that I should gain
> An interest in the Savior's blood?
> Died He for me, who caused His pain?
> For me, who Him to death pursued?
> Amazing Love, How can it be

That thou my God should die for me?

~

Refrain
Amazing Love! How can it be
That Thou, My God, should die for me!

~

He left His Father's throne above,
So free, so infinite His grace,
Emptied Himself of all but love,
And bled for Adam's helpless race,
'Tis mercy all, immense and free,
For, O my God, it found out me.

~

No condemnation now I dread,
Jesus and all in Him is mine!
Alive in Him, my living Head,
And clothed in righteousness divine,
Bold I approach the eternal throne,
And claim the crown, through Christ my own.[111]

It was amazing how we could feel and follow the mood of the moment. Everyone was so touched that there was total silence for about 30 seconds as everyone pondered what became theirs in salvation. Then all praise broke loose. Believers from all the nations of the world started to praise the work of Christ on the cross. Each culture praised God in their unique style, along with the cultural instrumental accompaniments they used on earth. After one culture's worship, another picked up with praise from their region of the world. Musical styles were representative of South America, Asia, Africa, the Middle East, Australia, Europe, and North America. God brought people to Himself from every corner of the world. They each expressed their praise to the Savior in their unique way to honor Him.

They presented song after song glorifying Lord Jesus and the love He showed in His death on the cross for hours. We drank in their music

---

[111] This text is in the public domain in the United States, written by Charles Wesley (1738)

because their heart expressed genuine and fresh praise of our Savior. Their unique presentation imprinted our hearts. Every song turned our focus to a different aspect of the passion and work of Christ on the cross and their transformation through reconciliation. In the holographic presentation, God showed us His uncut emotion and heartbeat for humanity, so we would never forget Jesus' accomplishment for us.

After the last national group sang, Jesus stood and shared His heart with us.

"My Father communicated with you how, through creation, you became ours. After we created humanity, you rebelled and went your own way. Sin caused you to incur your need for reconciliation in order to enter into a relationship with us. We wanted the truth of what happened on the cross to burn into your minds and emotions. I paid a great price to accomplish your reconciliation, and the Father wanted you to know the truth of what happened. We knew that allowing you to see it rather than hear about it would greatly impact you. He knew it would captivate our hearts in a way you would never forget. By my death, we reconciled the world to ourselves and made it possible for all humanity to be set free from their sins and become members of our family. As you know, all of you are here because of that very reason. Now you understand more fully, what I endured on the cross. That is what you accepted in salvation when you placed your faith in me and experienced reconciliation with us."

"By creation, we own you. By my death, I bought you. Today, we made known to you what happened in the creation and the crucifixion. We know you will never forget these two demonstrations for the rest of eternity. These presentations will be a stabilizing factor for your heart to remain devoted to us with understanding. We also want you to recognize our love and devotion to you fully. Knowing our love for you helps you remain loyal and devoted to us. My sacrifice adamantly affirms that truth beyond a shadow of a doubt."

It was now time for the angels to participate in the celebration. After Jesus finished, they could hold back no longer. One after another, the angels shared significant historical events in which they also played a part and in which they delighted watching God's dealings with man. They could not get over how He treated humanity in such gracious, merciful, and loving ways to bring them into salvation and then to help them live out the new life — several expressed in detail the wonder of God's gracious actions. God's steadfast love for the human race repeatedly amazed them through the centuries. Humanity didn't deserve it, yet it never changed God's devotion to them. Then several angels expressed their appreciation for how God allowed them the many opportunities to watch over man, protect him, and help them through difficult times.[112] They delighted in learning how God fulfilled Roman's 8:28-29 [113] as He took the bad, the evil, and the hurtful things of life when people really messed up, or when great difficulties entered their life, and God was able to bring good things into their lives, beyond description.

One angel after another shared their testimonies of specific details they delighted in learning about God as they served Him. They named individuals and spoke of particular incidents. It was interesting to hear of their confusion of why God allowed some trials and difficulties to happen in our lives before He brought about the blessings. They could not understand why God allowed certain things to happen until the reason became apparent. Many of them shared their joy of being able to be the bearer of blessings or protection to God's people. They delighted in man's joyfulness in those times.

Michael, the archangel, was the last one to share his heart. God wanted us to hear all of these stories so that this final message would have the maximum impact on our hearts. Michel stepped up and looked at every one of us, many with recognition. He broadly smiled as he

---

[112] Psalm 91:11 "For he will put his angels in charge of you, to guard you in all your ways."

[113] "And we know that in all things God works for the good of those who love him, who have been called according to his purpose. For those God foreknew he also predestined to be conformed to the image of his Son, that he might be the firstborn among many brothers and sisters."

began to speak. I think I detected a slight quiver of excitement in his lips.

"Many of you are just beginning to get to know God. We angels have served God faithfully since our creation. Just because we are sinless and perfect does not mean we know everything. Your condition is now like ours. Just as we learned much about God over the centuries, so you can count on learning so much more about Father God in the eons to come, and it will make your heads spin at times. Understanding God will not come automatically or even easily. Much of it will take a great deal of work and research, both alone and with groups, to learn what God wants for you to understand about Him."

"We want you to know that we continue to be amazed at what we learn about God every day that we serve Him. Some of you wonder how your stay could always be growing and learning and filled with joy. Let me tell you; we have not stopped our fascination with God. Every hour of every day, we learn something more about Him and His unfathomable ways and character. Every time we think we have seen it all, God astounds us with something new about the working out of His plans and ways that continues to amaze us. That gives us a greater desire and joy to serve Him and be in His presence. We love learning about Him and His ways, just as you have already discovered. We have been around Him for thousands of years, and none of us has grown tired of serving or learning about our great God. We want you to know that you will find the same to be true for you."

"We look forward to working together with all of you and becoming close friends. Do you know how many times we wanted to reveal ourselves to you as we protected you, helped you, and guided you through your difficult times? We look forward to seeing you, working with you, and even hanging out at the Living Water Café for some fellowship and maybe a sweet roll or a slice of pie. Yep, we like pie too."

We all broke into laughter at that. As we quieted, Michael just looked over us, enjoying the moment. You could tell that this great gathering touched him. The tell-tail signs of joy were whelming up within him. He could hardly contain himself. His feet started dancing a little to use his pent-up energy. With such love in his voice, he then shared his last thought.

> "We are headed into a time you have eagerly anticipated. No longer will you battle sin and its effects. Satan will no longer be able to peddle his lies and deceit or bring you harm. No more will you be deceived, feel lonely, or unloved again. Now you will learn the pleasure of serving God as we have. This joy will never grow old or leave you empty. It will be a constant wellspring of original praise to Father God, Lord Jesus, and the Holy Spirit."

Michael just stood there for a moment, and then everyone realized he had finished what he had to say. Not knowing what to do at first, we responded with a great round of cheers and applause, along with all the angels. We now understand more about our future. The angels shared how their faithful service helped them grow in their knowledge about the Lord. We knew that, as it took them centuries to learn the depths of the heart of God, it would also be a long time before we would catch up with the angels in our understanding of God's glory. It was something we were all anticipating eagerly.

Our thoughts were winding down, thinking that this last presentation concluded this grand celebration. Our hearts were full to overflowing. However, you can't predict what God is going to do next. Just when we thought it was over, God let us know there was one more important presentation for us. Jesus stood with all eyes fixed on Him.

Holy Spirit, Constant guide

"We have not concluded our presentation," Jesus continued. "This program would not be complete until the Holy Spirit presents Himself and His work. Over the ages, most people worshipped my Father and me. Often the Spirit's work was overlooked.

"Let me tell you about the Spirit's involvement in my life. When I took on humanity, I humbled myself by laying aside the independent use of my divine attributes. I submitted to the Holy Spirit and allowed Him to empower and guide me in all my works and teaching. Together we became one in my ministry. The incredible work I did was Holy Spirit-empowered. He taught me, gave me wisdom, and helped me understand the critical issues of life. His involvement is essential for you to know. Just as Holy Spirit empowered and enabled me to do God's ministry, so He did the same kind of work and ministry in you. He wanted to do more with each one, but most were not always cooperative or open. Now in eternity, you will find it very easy to live in constant dependence on the Holy Spirit, just as I lived my life before the cross. That will become your customary way of life.

"The Holy Spirit drew you to salvation. He convicted you of your sin, regenerated you, gave you His life to live, and equipped you to serve through your spiritual gifts. He empowered you as much as you allowed. The fruit of the Spirit is a picture of what we are like, and He sought to manifest His fruit in you, thus making you more like us. His filling allowed you to live a changed life, be more selfless, and understand our heart for the work of the ministry. He drew you into deeper fellowship with My Father and me. You all experienced His illumination as He opened your understanding to the truths and depths of the Bible. He made the truth clear to you so you could apply it to life and situations you faced daily. While sharing your faith, He helped you recall the Word of God. You would have been helpless to change without Him."

As Jesus talked about the work of the Holy Spirit, suddenly, He stopped in mid-sentence. With heightened senses, we eagerly anticipated what was about to take place. Then without saying a word, in His distinctive manner, the Spirit brought vivid visions to our minds. Each vision was unique and personal. We saw how the Spirit worked in our life, first preparing us to receive the gospel, then opening our minds to the truth. He showed us the multitude of ways He drew individuals to God. Some had a sweet and tender experience in coming to know the Lord. Many came as children, and surrender was easy. Others went through the fire before He got their attention. He used a million different ways to draw people to Jesus. Just as the Father loves variety in creation, the Spirit loves variety in how He works in lives. Each of us recognized the unique way we came to the Lord, and now the Spirit's leading was so obvious.

As each person's vision continued, we saw how the Spirit moved in our lives, empowering us to live as a Christian. Sometimes we responded submissively, but often we flatly refused with stubborn rejection and chose our selfish ways, but He never gave up on His children. He faithfully drew those who were willing into a deeper relationship with God. Each of us saw the positive effects of how the Spirit led us through our trials, testing, and hardships and what He accomplished through them. We saw how God used us to influence others. It was so heart-warming that in this concluding part of the presentation, He made it evident in our minds how proud He was and how deeply He loved us.

All of this happened in a fast-forward sort of way. It was all clear and fully comprehended by each. Everyone was in admiration of what the Spirit did in our lives and how, in an indiscernible manner, He revealed His work in us. Each of us gained a greater understanding of the unrelenting love the Spirit has for us. We will never again question His devotion with which He works in our life.

The Holy Spirit said nothing up to this point as He brought us to a comprehensive understanding of His work in us. What He said gave us a fuller understanding of how He works in our lives fully. He then spoke, not as Jesus did in His presentation. He communicated to us in our spirit. Everyone understood Him flawlessly. As I talked to people afterward, I found out He said the same thing to each of us.

"Here in heaven, you will experience both the fullness of a relationship with me and my continual work in your life. I will help and enable you to enjoy full fellowship with the Father and Son. We will be in constant fellowship with each other, which will allow you to have meaningful communion with others and us. My work in your life will help you understand yourself and your potential and empower you to express the fullness of the image of God. In this fellowship relationship, I will help you comprehend the secrets of heaven and the mind of God. Through me, you will always know the heart of my Father. Our communion will be the source of the fullness of joy in all your endeavors and worship. The more I work in your life, the closer we will be. I will be your constant friend and companion as you experience life and comprehend us more fully.

"When I tell you that you are in fellowship with us, do not take this lightly. We will allow you to enter our deepest thoughts and grand purposes. You will not automatically know things but learn them through exploration, study, contemplation, and practice. You will enjoy digging into the infinite depths of our knowledge. Just as a husband and wife grow in love and understanding of each other over the years, so your love will be ever growing in your relationship with God.

"As you delve into opportunities, we give you to serve, learn, and explore the things of God; your understanding will never stop seeking to know more about God and growing in your appreciation of Him. Learning deep truths will not be an end in itself but will find expression in your life and relationships. Truths will build on one another. What you learned 500 years ago will become more relevant when you learn other truths. We want you to grow in understanding us so you comprehend life as we do. From there, you will look for productive ways to put this new awareness into practice in creative lifestyles, in which you develop inspired worship and serve others. This work will not always be easy. Extracting these deep truths will take a lot of effort, thought, and commitment. You will struggle at times to come to that deeper understanding of our ways, and it may take many centuries to develop your new comprehension. You will also develop an intimate working relationship with me in this work. We also know you take great delight in discovering new ways to help others. All of what you learn will have a productive purpose, not just for you, but it will allow you to help others learn the benefits and applications of the truths you discovered. This learning will cause you and others to cultivate your relationship with us and worship in creative ways."

"You will always have access to my power, guidance, and wisdom. My wisdom will be your fountain for understanding the deep things of God. What you learn in the first million years will be foundational for what you learn in the eons to come. Just as it took time on earth to learn, it will take time and effort in heaven. I will reveal, in time, those profound truths of God and creation. As your understanding grows, so will your admiration of and love for God.

"You will learn other aspects of our image in you. Take, for instance, God's love. It will continue to develop in ways you never thought possible. You will grasp more fully the height, depth, breadth, and length of our love.[114] You will enjoy loving relationships with people in ways you never considered.[115] You will do difficult things for people without giving it a second thought because you will continue to develop a love for one another.

"Life here will allow you to derive an understanding of the depths of our love for you. Just as in a good marriage, love became more profound over the years, so you felt more a part of each other and were secure in your relationship. That will characterize your growing relationship with God. The longer you are here, the more you will expand your ability to experience and express our love. It will almost be imperceptible at times. You may take it for granted until I suddenly bring it to your attention. You will enjoy the delight of drawing closer to God and feeling such a part of Him.

---

[114] "For this reason I kneel before the Father, [15] from whom every family in heaven and on earth derives its name. [16] I pray that out of his glorious riches he may strengthen you with power through his Spirit in your inner being, [17] so that Christ may dwell in your hearts through faith. And I pray that you, being rooted and established in love, [18] may have power, together with all the Lord's holy people, to grasp how wide and long and high and deep is the love of Christ, [19] and to know this love that surpasses knowledge—that you may be filled to the measure of all the fullness of God" Ephesians 3:14-19

[115] "A new commandment I give to you, that you love one another. Just as I have loved you, you also must love one another. By this everyone will know that you are my disciples, if you have love for one another." John 13:24-35

"I have much more to tell you, but the rest will come as we work together and through the opportunities I give you. Therefore, this is an introduction to what my ministry will be in you. I am looking forward to our growing relationship in the coming ages.

"As we commence with eternity, I offer you a reminder that each of us, Father, Son, and Spirit, have invested heavily in every one of you. We do not take our relationship with you lightly. We want you to know that we are forever committed to you. That will never change. You can take that to the bank and count on it. I want you to remember the three essential truths we focused on today.

"The Father created you, and that reminds you of how intimately He understands you, as well as to whom you belong."

"Jesus redeemed you through His suffering and shed blood when you were our enemies. Thus He provided the only means of reconciliation for you."

"I drew you into the salvation relationship. In response to your faith, I regenerated you, indwelt you, and empowered you to live that new life we placed in you. I live in you now to allow you access to the fullness of life. My relationship with you will never diminish."

After the Holy Spirit finished, the celebration of worship and praise continued for the rest of the day. There were no more solos, but many wanted to sing, and the songs freely flowed as people broke into small groups. Many were composing new songs spontaneously. After hearing them a time or two, people caught on, sang, and improvised captivating counter melodies as they expressed their love for God. The freedom to express these songs spontaneously was so much fun. Some of the songs brought us to tears of joy, and others caused our spirits to rise, which brought us into delight and laughter in our celebration

It was a joyous time as we broke off from our group and walked home. We speculated about what God had in store for us. We also recapped what we liked best about the praise fest. God's presentation

153

caused us to experience both ecstasy and profound sorrow. It was so real and heart gripping. The whole production caused us to focus our praise and worship on our Creator, Savior, and Guide in life. It was fun walking from group to group, talking about the blessings of the day. Singing broke out spontaneously among many groups, and even though they were not singing the same songs, we found they were all harmonizing and making the praise so much more glorious. Oh, the Spirit is marvelous in His abilities.

Such an emotional event would wear us out on earth. Here, however, our stamina was boundless. We all had the desire and energy to continue. This experience was better than the Detroit Tigers winning the 1968 World Series![116]

Even though there would be many more praise festivals, none would be like this first one. We all fully experienced our new freedom of expression in these new heavenly bodies. Even though we felt close to God here, there was something about praising God within the whole community of believers. Corporate praise tends to draw us closer to Him. People did not want to leave; however, they melded into groups as time passed. Some went off by themselves to contemplate all that happened. They still needed their secluded time to process what took place. Heaven does not necessarily change all parts of our personality. Some process an event in solitude. Others like sharing with friends over coffee and a piece of pie or two.

"Let's go to the Water of Life Café," I suggested to Nancy and Lorrie. "They have the best banana cream pie."

Nancy said, "I want pumpkin. That has always been my favorite."

"That sounds good to me, too," said Lorrie. "I'm in! I want berry pie today. Jim, why don't you try some this time? You always get banana cream. Try something different."

---

[116] The Tigers winning the World Series was significant for Detroit. In 1967, Detroit was divided by the race riots and many neighborhoods were burned. The people were trying to get their new bearings on life. Winning the World Series brought hope to a hurting city.

Wow! Heaven is good and brings such pleasure. The best part of it is that the good times never stop, nor do any of our frailties or regrets ever haunt us again. This new land of peace, friendships, and purpose are far superior to anything we ever imagined.

It is good to be in heaven. I know I could never have thought of a better life. Say, are you planning to join us in heaven? Just a reminder, you cannot come unless you become reconciled with God. Hope to see you here. The Holy Spirit and Jesus leave you with a final word.

"The Spirit and the bride say, "Come!" And let the one who hears say, "Come!" Let the one who is thirsty come, and let the one who wishes take the free gift of the water of life."[117]

---

[117] Revelation 22:17

Readers Theater: Jesus the Redeemer

Introduction: The last chapter of the book A Glimpse into Heaven closes by assembling all the saints and angels in a great gathering to kick off eternity. The Father, Son, and Spirit present essential aspects of their work for humanity. The Father has a special presentation about creation, the Spirit on His work of drawing humanity to Himself, and His sanctifying work. The Son presents His work of redemption. Put yourself with all the redeemed in this grand opening event of eternity and listen to God's presentation to you about the work of redemption.

Jesus presented Himself to us seated on His throne. I shall never forget the immediate response by every person there. We fell to our knees and began to thank and worship Him for His great sacrifice that redeemed and reconciled us to God. Our time of thanksgiving turned into a time of praise and adoration, focusing on His willingness to lay down His life for us and the display of His abundant love. We included the very words written in Revelation about Him.

"You are worthy because you were slain,
and with your blood, you purchased for God persons
from every tribe and language and people and nation.
"Salvation belongs to our God,
who sits on the throne and to the Lamb.
Worthy are you, Lord Jesus, for you were slain.
"To you be praise and honor and glory and power, forever and ever!"

Jesus then stood, and everyone quieted immediately. Without saying a word, He raised His hand to call our attention to His part of the program. Jesus showed us the real-life holographic presentation of His arrest, trial, crucifixion, burial, and resurrection. The uniqueness of this presentation was that we not only saw what happened to Him, but He also allowed us to listen in on His thoughts as the events played out. Not only did we hear what He was thinking during the circumstances,

157

but we also felt some of His abandonment, betrayal, and the hurt of the unjust accusation, as He experienced the unmerciful beating by the Romans. Jesus also allowed us to experience bits of the suffering He faced that day at the hands of His Father. *"The Father laid on Him the iniquity of us all. It pleased the Lord to bruise him."*

Our understanding intensified so we could experience more realistically the anguish of Jesus bore. First, he took us to Gethsemane, and we heard his agony as he prayed, *"Father, release me from this cup."* We will **never** forget His arrest and seeing Him led away. We saw His eyes and felt his heart, as he looked at Peter right after his third denial. None of us condemned him, for we realized we all denied Christ many times during our life. It continued to worsen with the highly emotional ordeal of the beating Jesus suffered before going to the cross. We shuddered at his pain as they nailed Him to the cross. It was excruciating. We heard His accuser's insults as they spat abusive and demeaning remarks. We saw what He endured in the redemption process. We felt overwhelmed and full of sorrow as we silently watched him hanging there, suffering on our behalf.

Throughout the presentation, Jesus gave us a running commentary of His and the Father's thoughts as they freely shared their perspective. Jesus was suffering while His Father watched what His Son was enduring with total empathy. The significant events happened in real-time. We were all captivated as we drank in every word and felt their heart and concern. Father God shared with great emotion how crushed His heart was as Jesus not only suffered at the hands of man but also as He had to crush Jesus unmercifully for the punishment of our sins. We heard and felt the heart of God, and the passion they both had for the redemption of sinful man, and how His Son's suffering broke the Father's heart. Every one of us empathized with Him. As God was expressing His heart, our hearts moved with the most profound empathy.

No one was prepared for what was about to happen. As we watched Jesus suffering for our sins on that cross, unexpectedly, each of us became aware of every one of our sins and the agony it was bringing on our Savior. It was not just our significant sins, but in the

158

space of a few moments, God made us aware of every one of our failures, sins, and disobedience. Then something very unpredictable happened. Our sins moved from invisible thoughts to a visible display above each head. It was like a text balloon listing our every sin. In that instant, we remembered every one of those offenses. Jesus allowed us to experience just a taste of the suffering He was enduring for our sinfulness. The Father then caught us all off guard as He quickly reached out to every one of us and gathered our sins into one giant mass. It was bigger than anything we could imagine. His subsequent motion so stunned us we stood with mouths agape. The Father unmercifully crushed Jesus with the weight of our sins. As soon as He did that, Jesus cried out in heart-wrenching agony. Our hearts reacted as we empathized with His anguish caused by our sin. Never had anyone experienced such agonizing, indescribable pain. As terrible as it was, yet there was great beauty in what he was doing, for He was doing this because He loved us.

"My God, my God. Why have you forsaken me?" His hurt was deep. Never had either the Father or Son experienced any separation in their relationship. Both felt an emptiness that was unfathomable and foreign to their relationship. The Father had to turn His back on the Son, for He could not look on sin. He unrelentingly crushed His Son as He poured out His full wrath upon Him unmercifully. How could the Father do that? How could Jesus take it? It was because the innocent had to suffer for the guilty. Our sin was that offensive to the holy nature of God. We stood there stunned at the agony we heard in His groans and the pain we saw on His face as He suffered for us for the next three hours. His eyes revealed his excruciating pain. What we thought we understood earlier became almost more than we could endure as, once again, we remember Jesus crying out in the garden, *"Father, if it be your will, let this cup pass from me."* We now understood more fully how terrible and repugnant our sin was to God… to our Savior… to our Friend who willingly suffered and died for us.

While focusing on His suffering, something extraordinary happened. God was allowing us to tune into the thoughts of Jesus. He was not focusing on His anguish but had sorrow and joy as names were racing through his mind. He cited each name so fast we could only comprehend some names here and there, and they meant nothing to most of us. Every name, however, was significant to Jesus because he knew them. For the longest time, at the mention of each name, it brought a weight of sadness and sorrow over Jesus. The list went on for over an hour, and then his whole demeanor changed. His suffering did not let up, but you could sense the joy in Jesus' mind at the hearing of these names. It was then that the Holy Spirit opened our understanding. Those names that brought sadness are the ones who would reject His provision of salvation and spend eternity in hell. The ones who brought joy are the ones who would receive reconciliation and enter a relationship with God.[118] The name of every human came to His mind during that time of suffering. His agony emanated out of His love for all humanity. It was strange that amid our grief, we saw smiles come across each person's face as Jesus allowed each to hear their name as it raced through his mind.

While experiencing the heart and thoughts of Jesus, every one of us was stone-cold sober. How could we have joy during His agony? It was as if our hearts went dark. Each one experienced the hurt emotionally that our sin brought on Jesus. We watched Him as we internalized what He endured during those three hours of suffering. Jesus then cried out, *"It is finished!"* Immediately His pain ceased. Our souls were again at peace. He paid the ultimate price to gain our redemption.

We cringed as the soldier pierced His side, and the water and blood spilled to the ground. The soldiers stepped up and removed Jesus from the cross. Next, Joseph came and took Him to the tomb and lovingly laid Him inside. The reality of the moment captured our whole being. We watched the tomb from outside, remembering what had just happened. Later an angel took us inside to see Him lying dead on the hewn stone ledge. Jesus, the eternal God, the source of all life... lay lifeless. However, death could not hold Him. Suddenly a flash of light that was so bright and intense blinded us! The stone rolled away! Jesus

---

[118] Hebrews 12:2 (NIV) "...fixing our eyes on Jesus, the pioneer and perfecter of faith. For the joy set before him he endured the cross, scorning its shame, and sat down at the right hand of the throne of God."

victoriously rose to life. He exited the tomb triumphantly! Our Savior defeated death. **He was ALIVE!**

Watching the scene awakened anew the angel's feelings of that moment when they saw Jesus rise from the dead. Without any prompting, they rejoiced and celebrated as they did back then. They could not hold themselves back because of the joy that filled their heart.

We followed Jesus through His full passion, just as it happened. Each scene was a declaration of our appalling sinfulness and the suffering He endured for our sin. This presentation drew us into a fuller understanding of the cost of our disobedience and rebellion. He endeared our hearts to Him with a new and fuller reality. Because we entered His suffering by hearing His thoughts and feeling some of His pain that He endured for us, we knew more fully the enormous cost of our sin to God. None of us ever wanted to hurt God like that again.

In awe of Jesus' resurrection, what surprised me is that every one of us was still aware of our sin that caused His death and suffering. I shall never forget our reaction to the whole crucifixion scene. No one shed a tear, for we knew He removed our guilt because of that event. His death purchased for us complete and total forgiveness. God's goal was not to punish us for our sin but to enable us to remember the high cost of our sin to Him. God wanted us to know that He valued our relationship with us so much that He willingly made complete and total payment for our sin by laying down His life. Every one of us spontaneously responded in heartfelt appreciation, expressing thanks from the depths of our hearts. We erupted into spontaneous worship. We lauded Jesus, our Savior, for His finished work of redemption on the cross. We held nothing back as we sang and praised Him.

* * * * * * * * * * * *

For I received from the Lord that which also I delivered to you, that the Lord Jesus on the night in which he was betrayed took bread. When he had given thanks, he broke it and said, "Take, eat. This is my body, which is broken for you. Do this in memory of me."

In the same way, he also took the cup after supper, saying, "This cup is the new covenant in my blood. Do this, as often as you drink, in memory of me." For as often as you eat this bread and drink this cup, you proclaim the Lord's death until he comes. I Cor. 11: 23-26

Adapted from: "A Glimpse of Heaven – Imaging what heaven is like."

©James Olah: - jolah1968@gmail.com

Other books about eternity

I hope this book about heaven encourages you in your faith. My desire for this book is that people would gain realistic ideas by which they could imagine Heaven.

It is natural to wonder what happens after death; however, Heaven is not the only place people go when they die. As much as we do not want to think about that other place, it is also a reality. Being afraid of talking about hell does not change its existence. The problem most people have with hell is that they do not have a realistic understanding of what it is like in this place of torment.

Just as this book sought to give you a different understanding of heaven, my two books on hell also seek to open your awareness of this important topic.

Hell is a reality. Jesus, who created hell, affirmed the existence of this place many times in His teaching. Is hell just a burning place of constant punishment? Could the torment be something more than just literal flames? Is hell a place where internal burning is worse than external fire? Delve into this topic in my sequel book on eternal existence.

What in Hell is Happening?
A different perspective of hell's torment

"The Rich Man" is my most recent book and speaks of the Rich Man and Lazarus from Luke 16. Jesus said, "The Rich Man died and went to hell." The book takes you on a visit with the Rich Man as he describes what suffering is like there. We will explore words from the passage and other Bible teachings to understand how one might experience that type of suffering in hell.

About the Author

James Olah retired from the ministry after 39 years of service. He also served as a Hospice chaplain for three years. He enjoys the study of the word of God and delights in preaching, teaching, and writing.

It is fun to talk about exciting subjects, and heaven is one of those topics. When I preach the funeral of a believer, it is such a joy to be able to talk confidently about the person being in heaven. I come away from these funerals energized in my faith. After all, I just talked about my future home. I set my course for heaven, and the vehicle that will allow me to complete my journey is death.

This book follows the book I wrote about hell, "What in Hell is Happening?" It is indeed fitting and more pleasurable to address the topic of heaven. In both books, I seek to apply the Bible's teachings and bring the reader into a deeper understanding of each place. Though biblical in both books, the views are different than presented in most writings. Since the publication of this book, I have written another book on the afterlife. "The Rich Man," A first-person account from hell. It is about the Rich Man and Lazarus from Luke 16.

James lost his first wife, Nancy, to cancer after 43 years of marriage, and he features her story in this book. He married Lorrie in 2016 and lives in the Lansing, Michigan, area. He is available for speaking engagements.

Other Books by James Olah

What in Hell is Happening?
A different perspective of hell's torment
Christian Faith Series # 4

The Rich Man
A first-person account from hell
Based on the Rich man and Lazarus from Luke 16
Christian Faith Series # 6

Town of Salvation
How does Christianity differ from the Religions of the World?
What does the Bible teach about Salvation?
Book 1 of "Christian Faith Series

Keys for Growing Christians
A book of handy facts to help you understand the Christian faith,
How to live it, share it, and defend it.
Book 2 of Christian Faith Series

Helps for Christians
Issues facing the maturing Christian
Book 3 of Christian Faith Series

Getting to Know You
Questions to prepare for marriage
Questions to help understand a person better
Plus eight helpful relationship articles
Book 1 of Relationship Series

The Dynamics of Communication and Sex
Effective Keys to Preventing Relationship Breakdowns
Enjoying the Benefits of Maintaining a Healthy Sex Life in your Marriage
Book 2 of Relationship Series

What is the Tone of Your Communication?
How does the tone of voice affect your communication?
Book 3 of Improving Your Relationship Series

The Meeting Room
Online dating for beginners
Book 4 of Relationship series

Dating by Design
Dating intentionally to prepare for marriage
Dating helps for those who remarry
Book 5 of Relationship Series

Getting to Know You
Questions to prepare for marriage
Questions to help understand a person better
Plus eight helpful relationship articles
Book 1 of Relationship Series

The Dynamics of Communication and Sex
Effective Keys to Preventing Relationship Breakdowns
Enjoying the Benefits of Maintaining a Healthy Sex Life in your Marriage
Book 2 of Relationship Series

What is the Tone of Your Communication?
How does the tone of voice affect your communication?
Book 3 of Improving Your Relationship Series

The Meeting Room
Online dating for beginners
Book 4 of Relationship series

Dating by Design
Dating intentionally to prepare for marriage
Dating helps for those who remarry
Book 5 of Relationship Series

How Fast? How Far? How Big?
Fun Facts for Kids about Speed, Distance,

and Size in Our Solar System and Universe.
Trivia to Amaze Your Friends
1 - Children's Fun Learning Series

Sploring with Papa
A fun Story of a Grandson and Grandpa exploring (sploring)
Rail Road Tracks and an Old Barn, as told by Trinity
2 - Children's Fun Learning Series

Purchase digital copies from Kindle, iBooks, and Nook

Please take the opportunity to write a review of the book.

If this book has been a help to you in getting excited about heaven, the author invites you to share your thoughts with him.
Jolah1968@gmail.com

Made in the USA
Columbia, SC
23 February 2023

12770594R00091